Praise for
You're Gonna Make It

"A good plan almost never survives the blow of the enemy. We need more than a plan; we need a strategy—and the resilience—to keep going when our plan capsizes. Strategy is exactly what you will find in the pages of this book. Daniel will hand you the tools to persevere when life hits so hard you want to quit. *You're Gonna Make It* will give you the kind of resilience that doesn't just help you survive hardship but also helps you bounce back even stronger."

—LEVI LUSKO, lead pastor of Fresh Life Church and bestselling author

"Sometimes life seems so unfair, so hard. Maybe you're terrified of the future or find it hard to believe that you will ever really be happy again. If that's you, then *You're Gonna Make It* is a must-read. Daniel Fusco lays out a thoughtful, practical guide to finding true hope in the suffering, fear, worry, and everyday pressures of life. In a time when hope seems to be in relatively short supply, Daniel encourages us to lean into the hope we have in Jesus, despite our circumstances, and reminds us that God is still in control. Jesus will get us through whatever we are facing today."

—GREG LAURIE, senior pastor of Harvest Church and evangelist for Harvest Crusades

"Daniel Fusco has written another timely and practical book that can lift a person from the deepest low to a thrilling triumph. He teaches us a hope that puts the grit in perseverance!"

—BISHOP DALE C. BRONNER, DMIN, founder and senior pastor of Word of Faith Family Worship Cathedral and author of *Power Principles*

"Overthinking is one of the biggest causes of unhappiness. My beloved friend Daniel Fusco expertly guides us, in a thoroughly biblical way, in what it looks like to break free from our 'what-if' mental prisons. *You're Gonna Make It* is a compelling read, spilling over with gospel truths. This book gives so much hope for true, God-honoring change."

—RASHAWN COPELAND, founder of Blessed Media and author of *No Turning Back*

"This incredible book leads us on a journey of trusting God in chaotic seasons. Daniel's insights and experiences are perfectly woven through the threads of this book. If you desire to unlock the resilience inside you and learn about God's path for your life, *You're Gonna Make It* will not disappoint!"

—TIM TIMBERLAKE, bestselling author of *The Power of 1440* and senior pastor of Celebration Church

"*You're Gonna Make It* is a ray of light. Daniel unveils the secret to finding hope in the midst of life's uncertainties. If you're wondering what it takes to become resilient for times like these, read this book!"

—CAREY AND TONI NIEUWHOF, podcasters, speakers, bestselling author (Carey) of *At Your Best*, author (Toni) of *Before You Split*

"Daniel Fusco, as only he can, brings a timely message in *You're Gonna Make It*. It will encourage and challenge you in the most life-giving way. All of us have experienced the mess of life. The gift of resilience is the key to not just surviving but also thriving through it all. Daniel is one of the most brilliant pastors and Bible teachers I know, but what I love most about him is his heart to encourage people. This book will unlock resilience and release hope in your life."

—BANNING LIEBSCHER, Jesus Culture founder and pastor

"I wish I could tell you that once you become a Christian, life is easy. But that's not true. Life is still hard, but God is still good. In *You're Gonna Make It,* Daniel Fusco teaches us to be resilient like Jesus. This book is chock-full of powerful life principles that will transform your hard seasons into miracles."

—MATT BROWN, evangelist, author of *Truth Plus Love,* host of *Think Eternity with Matt Brown* podcast, and founder of Think Eternity

"In a world embroiled in chaos, consternation, pain, and uncertainty, Daniel Fusco serves up gospel-driven joy for life and hope for the future. At a time in our culture when many are suffering and grappling with so much, Fusco offers a powerful reminder that God can do extraordinary things with our lives when we trust Him to navigate us through the storms. *You're Gonna Make It* is a must-read for the times in which we're living."

—BILLY HALLOWELL, author and digital host, CBN News

"*You're Gonna Make It* is a how-to guide not just for surviving hard times but also for *thriving* in the midst of them. Daniel Fusco offers practical wisdom that will keep you anchored to unconditional hope no matter what you're facing. Whether it's a financial mess, health crisis, or difficult relationship, this book will offer you hope and joy for your journey."

—ROMA DOWNEY, Emmy-nominated actress, producer, and *New York Times* bestselling author

"*You're Going to Make It* by Daniel Fusco is the book everyone needs right now—a perfect antidote for those who feel stuck in the middle of life and don't know which way to seek help. Daniel's own story, along with his biblical perspective, is sure to bring you to a place beyond what you could have imagined: Ephesians 3:20. While reading, I thought about past times I could have used this book and applied it to my own life, to gain the wisdom that comes from this kind of perseverance. Thank you, Daniel, for writing this book. Everyone needs to read it!"

—SHAWN BOLZ, author, pastor, TV host, podcaster, @shawnbolz, www.bolzministries.com

YOU'RE
GONNA
MAKE IT

YOU'RE GONNA MAKE IT

Unlocking Resilience
When Life Is a Mess

DANIEL FUSCO
with D. R. Jacobsen

WATERBROOK

Published in the United States by WaterBrook, an imprint of Random House, a division of Penguin Random House LLC.

WATERBROOK® and its deer colophon are registered trademarks of Penguin Random House LLC.

Library of Congress Cataloging-in-Publication Data
Names: Fusco, Daniel, author. | Jacobsen, D. R. author.
Title: You're gonna make it: unlocking resilience when life is a mess / Daniel Fusco with D.R. Jacobsen.
Description: Colorado Springs: WaterBrook, [2022] | Includes bibliographical references.
Identifiers: LCCN 2021058271 | ISBN 9780593192689 (trade paperback) | ISBN 9780593192696 (ebook)
Subjects: LCSH: Resilience (Personality trait)—Religious aspects—Christianity.
Classification: LCC BV4597.58.R47 F87 2022 | DDC 233/.5—dc23/eng/20220224
LC record available at https://lccn.loc.gov/2021058271

Printed in the United States of America on acid-free paper

waterbrookmultnomah.com

9 8 7 6 5 4 3 2 1

First Edition

Book design by Diane Hobbing.

SPECIAL SALES Most WaterBrook books are available at special quantity discounts when purchased in bulk by corporations, organizations, and special-interest groups. Custom imprinting or excerpting can also be done to fit special needs. For information, please email specialmarketscms@penguinrandomhouse.com.

To Pastor Bill and Betty Ritchie and the entire Crossroads Community Church family—past, present, and future—for being extraordinary.

FOREWORD

I need a little hope . . .

I remember thinking this more than a few times in 2020.

My world was turned upside down because, like so many others, I had important things I needed to do that just evaporated overnight. I had tours canceled. And my feature film, *I Still Believe,* which tells part of my life story, opened in theaters right before everything *everywhere* shut down. Talk about a gut punch.

As weeks turned into months that year, I started feeling as though I was losing my grip on what I was even called to do. Or at least what I thought I was called to do. What was I supposed to be doing? Did any of this matter? I felt like I didn't even know anymore. I was losing hope.

Now, I had felt this way many years prior because I had lived through some of the hardest stuff anyone faces. I lost my first wife to cancer, and through that experience, I learned how to dig down deep and find the dedication to say, "I trust You, God."

I wrote a song called "I Still Believe" during that season of my life (which is what the movie is all about, by the way), and a big part of that writing process was trying to find a way to unlock resilience in the middle of the struggles—trying to find hope when everything inside me was shouting, *I just can't do this anymore!*

My friend Daniel Fusco brings so much hope and joy to me—and to the world through his ministry. This book you're holding right now drills down on this key ingredient to thriving: *hope*. It's the missing piece in many of our stories. *You're Gonna Make It* is not just a catchphrase; it's *practical*. Real talk. It's something we can explore and apply. Take it from someone who's been there: This is street-level wisdom. And I'm thankful for a tool like this to comfort others around me.

The more I read this book, the more I discover the deep spiritual gold. After everything I've been through in my life, I've come to realize that hustling or trying harder isn't gonna bring us hope—at least not *lasting* hope. And I don't know about you, but I want to experience real hope. I want to be resilient in the face of pressure, stress, and pain. And I want my life to point people to a real solution, a solution that changes individuals, families, and communities from the inside out.

I've always tried to use my experiences to help people learn to say, "I trust You, God," even in the middle of the hardest trials. And trusting God is something we can do better—when we learn what it looks and feels like to rise above.

With this book, I hope you enjoy discovering the depth of Jesus's love for you and the many powerful ways you can find deep, lasting hope for today and tomorrow.

Because at the end of it all, Jesus is still on the throne and all His promises are true. No matter what we're walking through.

Jeremy Camp
Christian artist, songwriter, and author

CONTENTS

YOU'RE
GONNA
MAKE IT

1

UNLOCKING RESILIENCE

RingRingRing!

I groaned, rolled over, and stuffed my head under the pillow. My machine would pick up the call. The sun wasn't even up yet, so that meant it was way too early for *me* to be up. I needed every minute of sleep I could get.

Silly East Coasters, I thought. *It's been three years!*

After completing college in my native state of New Jersey, I picked up and moved west. I spent a few years living in beautiful Southern Oregon before transplanting to the San Francisco Bay Area, living in Marin County. But I understood the deal: right now, three time zones east of me, my friends and family would be having their morning coffee, thinking they had a nice chunk of time to call a buddy. Problem was that if the buddy was me, they'd wake me up because of the time difference. This was pretty common on the weekends,[1] but today was a weekday! I hoped if my machine picked up enough calls that maybe everyone would figure it out and start calling me after work. Either that

---

[1] Which was bad enough for a young lad such as myself.

or I'd have to go straight Jersey on them, throwing down the gauntlet and saying, "No one is allowed to call before lunch!"[2]

After five rings, my machine clicked on. Remember, this was when phones still had a cable attached to the wall and there was another mysterious box that recorded your messages for you.[3] I had the volume down, but I knew the person on the other end was hearing the smooth sound of a certain Daniel Fusco breaking down for them the exact info I wanted them to leave me so that I could call them back. *Finally, back to sleep.*

Except the phone rang again. My machine picked it up again. *Why is someone bugging me so much? What's so important?*

I was in my early twenties, working my first real job (in an office building with a watercooler and copier room and everything), so getting out of bed on a Tuesday before my alarm went off at seven-thirty was a definite no-go.[4]

When the phone rang for the fourth time, I reached over and turned up the volume on the answering machine. "Pick up the phone, Daniel! Pick up the phone! C'mon, pick up, pick *up*!"

Yikes. That did *not* sound good. I reached past the ma-

---

[2]   I kid. If you know me at all, you know I would never yell at someone over the phone. I'm just letting you in here and sharing my inside voice with you.

[3]   If memory serves me correctly, I think mine still had a little cassette tape in it. No age jokes, please!

[4]   If you've seen me in person, you know beauty sleep is one of the only things keeping other people from reporting a Sasquatch sighting when I go hiking.

chine and grabbed the handset. "What?" I grunted, rolling back onto my pillows.

"Where's Chris?" asked the voice. It was my buddy Rob from Jersey. Chris was a mutual friend.

"Chris?" I repeated.

"Yes, where's Chris?" Now Rob was yelling. "Chris works in the Towers, right?"

What in the world is he talking about? "Bro, it's like six in the morning!" I protested. "How the heck am I supposed to know where Chris is? I don't even know who he's working for these days. What's going on?"

"Wait, you don't—oh man, you're three hours behind. You're not gonna believe this. Go turn on a television *right now*. Any channel. There's a huge thing going on with the Twin Towers, and I think Chris works there."

Click.

I sat up, stunned. Nothing was making sense. And to make matters worse, I didn't have a TV.[5]

So I found the next best thing and cranked up the radio on my alarm clock. The news anchors were talking about some sort of accident at the Twin Towers and an explosion. I didn't catch the whole story, but just the tone of their voices was chilling. I jumped into sweats, pulled on a hoodie and some flip-flops, and raced out the door to my car. I had to get to a television and find out more. Who did I know who worked in the Towers? I still had tons of friends and family back East, including a bunch who worked in or around Manhattan, but how many were at the Towers?

---

[5] Pretty common now, but back then "cutting the cord" wasn't a thing. I wasn't trying to be cool—I was just a guy without a television!

I left my street and turned onto the main road. *Does my buddy Chris work there? I don't know.*

There was a strip mall up ahead. *I think my brother-in-law might work at a law firm with an office in the Twin Towers.*

I drove around and around. Nothing was open.

Finally, I found a chain diner, open for breakfast. *I seriously don't know where anyone I know works!*[6]

My stomach was clenching and unclenching as I parked and ran inside the diner.

And I watched in horror as I saw the Twin Towers coming down.

How are we going to make it through this? I wondered.

* * *

If you are one of the majority of Americans today who can remember 9/11, I'm sure you could tell me *exactly* where you were that day.

As I watched the news on TV and talked with family and friends that day, I learned my brother-in-law did work in the Towers. But he wasn't there that morning. His was one of the many miraculous stories we heard later. Because he'd worked late the night before, his boss told him to come in a bit later the next day. But his firm lost dozens of people. My buddy Chris *wasn't* there that morning,[7] thank God.

---

[6]   This all happened before social media, and I didn't have a clue where anyone worked.

[7]   It turns out he didn't even work there. My buddy Rob had been mistaken.

Still, even without knowing anyone who lost their life there, I knew in my gut that I'd never forget those attacks. And the same way we remember 9/11, others remember exactly when they heard about the space shuttle *Challenger* exploding or the assassination of John F. Kennedy or the day that will live in infamy, the attack on Pearl Harbor. There's just something about certain catastrophic events that sticks in our minds and refuses to leave.

And it's in the face of these events that we wonder how people are going to make it through it all.

Fast-forward almost twenty years to March 2020, when I was traveling to Arizona to teach at a conference and then preach in Albuquerque, New Mexico.

I know: 2020. *That* year.

By March, all of us had heard of the novel coronavirus, but most felt safe enough, insulated enough, to spend more time joking about it being named after the classic Cinco de Mayo beer (Corona) than worrying about what it might do to our communities, economy, and loved ones. I was at the airport in Albuquerque, ready to fly home, when my assistant, Diana, called me and asked, "Hey, do you want me to change your flight? You guys have to lay over in Seattle."

I made my puzzled face, which of course my assistant couldn't sense, so I elaborated. "Ummm . . . huh?"

Diana, in her usual patient way, explained that Seattle, at that moment, was at the center of the quickly growing Covid-19 outbreak, and the SeaTac airport was a busy layover spot for world travelers.

"Listen," I told her, "we'll be okay. Thanks for thinking of us, but don't worry about it."

My confidence wasn't based on anything, by the way! I

had no idea what the risk was, but I *did* know that I didn't want to change my flight. Meanwhile, the guy I was traveling with was using his phone to shop for masks and hand sanitizer on eBay and telling me everything was sold out. When we boarded our flight, I noticed people were pulling their shirts up over their mouths and noses, so I did the same. The reality was setting in. Something frightening was happening that I didn't have any control over. Something big.

Less than twenty-four hours later, the president recommended that everyone stay home for the next few weeks. At Crossroads Community Church, where I'm the pastor, we sent our staff home and closed in-person services for what we hoped would be a few weeks.[8]

Gosh, what in the world is going on? How are we ever going to make it through this madness?

* * *

Meanwhile, back at home, some folks who were dear to my heart were in trouble.

Pastor Bill Ritchie and his wife, Betty, are two heroes of our family. Bill became my friend when I was a young pastor. He was leading a megachurch just north of Portland, Oregon, while I pastored only a hundred people in a rented building, and he was always available to take the time to talk with me and advise me. Bill's actually the one who invited me to Crossroads more than a decade ago to be his successor.

In early February 2020, Betty got very sick. She was rushed to the emergency room, then transferred to another hospital,

---

[8]   Our math wasn't great on that!

but she kept getting worse. No matter what tests they ran or what they treated her with, the doctors couldn't help her. Soon she was admitted to the intensive care unit and put on a ventilator and given a feeding tube.

I know most of you are reading this and thinking, *He's gonna tell us she had Covid-19!*

You're right. She did.[9]

But nobody knew it then. The doctors were at a total loss. A couple of times, things got so bad for Betty that she flat-lined and a team had to rush in and resuscitate her. More than once, a doctor reached out to Bill to talk about his wife's options for end-of-life care.

I love how Bill responded. Each time, he said something like, "There ain't no way. I believe in God. I'm hoping in God. My entire life I have been talking to people about Jesus Christ. My life is a life that is nothing if not optimistic. There's got to be more that we can do. We don't quit. End of story."

And together with his son-in-law (who's a doctor), his daughter-in-law (who's a lawyer), and his other kids (who are all very gifted), they advocated for a care plan that would eventually help bring Betty back to health. It took thirty-five days in ICU, but Betty did come home.

I was in tears watching the video online as Betty's friends and family lined her street with their cars, waving and honk-ing their horns. Balloons were tied to almost every tree. As Betty and Bill drove slowly down the road, their smiles got wider and wider and wider.

Listen, I know many people who have tried everything

---

[9] But keep in mind that this was happening before they even had tests for Covid-19 where we lived.

possible and still were not able to survive a tough disease, including my own mother, who passed away at forty-nine years young. I've attended those funerals. I've led those funerals. So I want to be really clear about why I'm bringing up Bill and Betty's story. In this book, we are talking about resilience. We are talking about how to make it through the messiest things. Resilience is fueled by hope and grit. And I see the way Bill handled his wife's illness as a model for any of us trying to persevere through suffering, fight the battle against fear and worry, and even begin to thrive in the midst of constant stress.

Bill put his hope in what God could do. He married that hope to the grit he had. And, ultimately, something beautiful happened: Resilience flowed. See, grit isn't about mindlessly toughing it out. Instead, it's about persevering toward a good goal and not giving up until you get there, because you know it'll be worth it.

Bill's hope drove him into action, and that hope sustained him as he battled. His resilience and passion to keep Betty alive—his commitment to never quit, never stop—is what gave her a chance to survive. And by God's grace, she made it through.

*   *   *

So as Bill and Betty were fighting Covid-19, we all were battling the fallout from this crazy, unexpected lockdown. Across the country, many people were getting furloughed or, worse yet, losing their jobs. People were catching the coronavirus and dealing with the symptoms, as well as the lingering effects. And politics began to rage like never before.

I bring all this up because my church family, Crossroads Community Church,[10] all of a sudden couldn't hold in-person services. Like many other states, ours was pretty much shut down. Many of you experienced it too. It was so frustrating. And what we hoped would be a few weeks became a few months . . . and then a few more months. After I talked with people about what was going on and what we were feeling, I asked God for a fresh outlook. I prayed for clarity on how we could deal with this unprecedented season. I realized we needed God to speak. We needed a word of hope that was real and that we could act on. We felt so out of control—what could we even do? Most of us have never lived through anything like this.[11] But the Lord wanted to work on us and help us grow through that season.

What I knew I needed to tell the Crossroads family is that we were gonna make it through this. And I want you to hear that as well. You are gonna make it!

So I started looking through my Bible and grabbing hold of verses that spoke about how to hang on and hope, verses about perseverance and grit. And I know I wasn't the only one searching for answers! As the months went by and we weren't meeting in person as a church family, we doubled down on reaching out to people on the phone[12] and caring

---

[10] We're at 7708 NE 78th Street, in Vancouver, Washington. We'd love to have you stop by! Or join us for weekend services online at https://crossroadschurch.net.

[11] And even now, the pandemic is still with us and we have to figure it out as we go.

[12] I told our staff that we were "going analog"—old-school ministry still works!

for them digitally. And I spent many hours meeting with pastors who were trying to help their church families navigate extraordinary circumstances.

We heard more and more stories of how people were trying to live through this unprecedented time, and we realized two things: One, plenty of folks were trying to make it through without Jesus and needed to meet Him or come back to Him. Two, plenty of people who already knew Jesus still seemed to be missing something. They were surviving—sometimes barely—but definitely not thriving. It was like the wheels were falling off, one by one, and there wasn't a plan to get things repaired and functioning again, let alone back to full speed.

Basically, hope was in short supply. It still is.

And for those who had hope, many still were struggling as they tried to translate that hope into victory.

We all realized as the pandemic went on that the grit and determination to seek out hope—and then to live it out—is a rare commodity. That's why I decided to write this book, as life is so messy and I want to help people hope again.

Things rarely work out the way we want them to, so we need more than a hope mindset; we need to combine that mindset of hope in Jesus with character and choices that are gritty. I've heard it said that grit is passion and perseverance toward long-term goals. The way author Angela Duckworth has described it is this: Grit means following a consistent compass, not a bunch of random, fleeting fireworks.[13] Passion for Christ is our start and our finish—loving our Savior

---

[13]   This is a loose synopsis from Angela Duckworth, *Grit: The Power of Passion and Perseverance,* Scribner, loc. 919, Kindle.

and being loved by Him. We want to live out and experience 1 John 4:19, loving Him because He first loved us, over and over and over. *And*—not *but*—along with that passion and love, we want to develop a perseverance, a steadfastness, a stick-to-it-iveness, a git-er-done-and-then-some work ethic.

When that happens, all inspired by the Holy Spirit? We make it. We struggle. We learn. We grow. We make it. And as we journey, we learn how to unlock resilience.

I like to use a little equation: *Hope + Grit = Unstoppable Resilience.*

And the outcome of that? Well, no matter the details of what happens, in God we can know that *we are gonna make it*. What I want you to hear as we close is this: In suffering, in worry, in fear, and in stress, if you hope in Jesus and live with grit, you *will* come out better on the other side.

You won't just overcome an obstacle or three—you'll *be* an overcomer.

Remember, the apostle Paul empowers us when he confirms that we are *more* than conquerors through Christ who loves us (see Romans 8:37). We are *overwhelmingly victorious.*

Now we must dig in and talk about it. I need to explore this and to trust in this good news as much as anyone. So let's begin our journey together.

2

PERSEVERING IN THE MIDST OF SUFFERING

To suffer is as human as to breathe.

–Albus Dumbledore,
Harry Potter and the Cursed Child

Life is full of hard things. As one of my friends likes to say, "Doo-doo occurs."[1] We've all experienced it. Unemployment. Broken relationships. Chronic pain. And there's something about suffering that can make it feel as though we're handcuffed to a treadmill and the only thing that changes is how fast we're forced to run.

I wouldn't be surprised if you're nodding and saying, "So true," from wherever you're reading this.[2]

---

[1] I hope you're not offended by that. I tried to soften it as much as I could. But it does happen.

[2] Or like we say in church, "Amen."

And whenever we find ourselves in the middle of a painful season, with no end to the suffering in sight, we tend to cry out.

This isn't fair!
Why do I have to go through this?
God, not again!

Questions and outcries like this are natural. But that doesn't mean they're welcome or easy.

Everybody hurts.

–R.E.M., from the album *Automatic for the People*

The thing is, since we're human, suffering is inevitable, even though answers to why are sometimes hard to find.

It doesn't matter our age or stage of life. We're going to get hurt. We're going to suffer. Unfortunately, that's just the way life is. I wish I could change that for you, but I can't. I also know that there is a treasure found when we unlock resilience. It's something that the world needs, that our souls long for, and that gives glory to God. Resilience is extraordinarily Christlike.

Our culture is obsessed with trying to sweep suffering under the rug. We feel the pressure to plaster on a smile and pretend everything is great. Especially in the Christian community, right? But the reality is that suffering is the norm. The individual details will be different. The pain will touch distinct places in each of our hearts.

But all of us will hurt.

So what is suffering, exactly? It's more than the inconvenience of a flat tire on the way to work.[3]

In this book, when we talk about suffering, in general we're talking about entire *seasons* of pain—weeks, months, or even years when we feel abandoned, crushed down, or beaten up, sometimes so distant from God that we can hardly remember ever being close. Have you been filled up with pain to the point that you can't feel anything else? Almost can't imagine anything else?

That's the danger point: when our once-soft souls are at risk of hardening like concrete.[4] When we are born, we are wide open and excited about . . . everything. But then life happens and we find ourselves listless and lacking joy. This is a big issue. Sometimes we make it through things but lose ourselves, our humanity, in the process. We end up cold and bitter, almost inhuman. How do we endure that? How do we win the battles—never mind the war—when we can't even see past our own pain?

In Buddhism's Four Noble Truths,[5] the first truth is that *life is full of suffering.* True—and a bummer! But as discouraging as suffering can be, what if I told you it has a purpose?

And what if I told you that God has a unique plan that—crazy as it sounds, I know—can unfold only *through* our seasons of suffering?

---

[3]   Or the inconvenience of bad Wi-Fi when you're working from home.

[4]   You might be asking, "How do I know if my heart is hard like concrete?" Don't worry—if you're asking the question, it's not.

[5]   Quoting Buddha's teaching might seem strange, but it's not really Buddha's truth in the first place. Suffering is all throughout the Bible. All truth, at the end of the day, is God's truth.

Suffering has been stronger than all other teaching, and has taught me to understand what your heart used to be. I have been bent and broken, but—I hope— into a better shape.

–Charles Dickens, *Great Expectations*

And what if I told you that suffering doesn't have the last word?

I hope that sounds like good news. Talking about suffering is not very popular, especially when you say it's part of God's plan. But as we continue this story, I'll do my best to prove that suffering isn't the end of the story.

When we're suffering, it can feel like we're in the middle of the ocean, being tossed around by waves. We desperately need something we can wrap our arms around. Something we can cling to. Some good news.

That's where hope comes in.

Sometimes this hope is a settled confidence that God can bring good out of the challenging issues we're facing. Have you felt that before? That kind of hope is a deep-down belief that God isn't finished with us yet—that no matter what we're going through, God will have the last word.

Like a small light leading us out of a dark place, hope can change everything.

I consider that the sufferings of this present time are not worthy to be compared with the glory which shall be revealed in us.

—the apostle Paul, Romans 8:18

Other times the only thing we're confident in is that things will keep getting worse. And then we need something a bit different from hope. Not *instead* of hope, but *in addition* to it. We need to persevere. To hold on in hope or even to hold on against all hope. To keep pushing ahead, even when everything around us—and maybe even inside us—is telling us to give up.

In this book, I'm calling that resilient, tough quality *grit*. And it is something we all need right now.

Grit isn't just blind hard work without direction. And it isn't just having that direction either. Grit means hoping in something *and* working toward that thing.

For Christians, that hope is in Jesus, and choosing to walk toward Him every day can transform even the most severe suffering.

Listen, just clenching our teeth and hanging on isn't going to solve suffering!

But what grit does is provide us with the ability to see God's perfect plans, *even as they grow out of the dirt and ashes of our suffering.* It is this revelation that helps us not only survive on this journey we call life but also thrive in the midst of life's messiness.

3

DON'T WASTE
THE HARD THINGS
ROMANS 8:18-39

Jesus never promised us a life where everything would be easy. But even in suffering, He is doing a unique work. There is no waste in God's kingdom. Everything is purposeful, and God uses all things for your good and His glory.

I can remember almost exactly when I realized that life isn't always perfect.

It was the summer after my first year of college. I was attending Rutgers University in my home state of New Jersey. And that summer, my mom just wasn't quite right. She had this little nagging cough and found herself periodically lacking balance. Then one morning at breakfast, she began randomly dropping her fork. Something was going on. Early one morning, my dad took her to a doctor appointment, and they were gone the entire day. That night, my father walked in the door without my mom. She was still at the hospital.

"Danny," he told me, beginning to weep, "your mom has cancer."[1]

That was the beginning of an excruciating journey—for my mom more than the rest of us, but also for me, my sisters, my father, and my grandparents. There were seasons of radiation and chemo and allergic reactions to medicines, and through it all wove a dark thread of deep dread. No one expected my mom to pull through. Not with the type of cancer she had. Not with the treatments they had twenty years ago. All too soon, she passed away.

To be honest, up until that point in my life, things had been pretty easy. Beautiful even. Life had been unfolding how I'd expected it to: hanging with family and friends, screaming our heads off at football games, watching the sun go down at the shore.[2] I had so many good memories! And it seemed like I'd just keep building many more. Then all of a sudden I saw, I *felt,* how messy real life is.

That's only become clearer to me as I've gotten older. Life is so, *so* messy. But I always say that life is messy but Jesus is real.[3] And He has an amazing way of meeting us in the middle of our messes.

---

[1]   I tell this story in more detail in my book *Honestly: Getting Real About Jesus and Our Messy Lives.*

[2]   And when you are in Jersey, you are always going "down" to the shore, both literally and figuratively.

[3]   I pray I never get tired of saying this and that you never get tired of hearing it, because until heaven, this will always be the case. Always!

WE'RE IN TROUBLE

Unfortunately, those of us who are followers of Jesus are susceptible to a certain temptation: believing that Jesus will make everything go perfectly for us.[4]

We might not say it out loud, but we kind of expect it, don't we? We think that because we prayed for that job, we will *definitely* get it. Or because we are God's children, we won't get into serious conflicts with people. Or because we know Jesus and He is the Great Physician, our physical healing is inevitable. All things work together for good, right?

I mean, right?

That may be true, but we don't get to pick what "good" looks like. The Bible never says that if we believe in Jesus, everything will come up roses. In fact, the opposite is true. And if you want to talk about promises, well, Jesus actually promises us that in this world, we will have trouble! He puts it this way in John 16:33: "In the world you will have tribulation; but be of good cheer, I have overcome the world."

So we're always going to face things that are tough. That's not always easy to accept, is it? That's why the apostle Paul, writing to the church in Corinth, said,

> Therefore we do not lose heart. Even though our outward man is perishing, yet the inward man is being renewed day by day. For our light affliction, which is but for a moment, is working for us a far

---

[4]   Ultimately, it is true that it does go perfectly for us: perfectly the way God intends. Here I mean perfectly how we want it to go.

more exceeding and eternal weight of glory, while we do not look at the things which are seen, but at the things which are not seen. For the things which are seen are temporary, but the things which are not seen are eternal. (2 Corinthians 4:16–18)

We are suffering. All of us. It's very real and very painful. But the reason I'm writing this book is to help us hang on. And not just to hang on but to be victorious. I realize that victory looks different in different types of suffering. But, ultimately, victory is declared when we don't lose heart, so don't lose heart! Make sure you internalize what I just said. Do not lose heart, please. We will suffer, yes. But the glory God has prepared for us makes any suffering a "light affliction" in comparison.

If that sounds dismissive of present suffering, remember what Paul endured: beatings, whippings, imprisonment, shipwreck, public scorn, and a few very public assassination attempts. I mean, imagine that. There were basically John Wick–style assassins trying to kill Paul back in biblical times![5] Yet he still kept his eyes on the prize. Even as *outward* life got worse, his *inward* life—what we might call his heart and his relationship with Jesus—got better and better.

That's what he's imploring us to do as well: Stop denial. See life clearly—*real* life. This isn't about pretending we don't see suffering around us or that we aren't suffering ourselves.

---

[5] If you don't believe me, read the second half of the book of Acts. But those assassins really weren't John Wick–style, because they couldn't get the job done.

Instead, it's about seeing what's in front of us now as temporary and understanding that many unseen things are eternal.

This is when we decide if we believe that this stuff we read in the Bible and see in the lives of the apostles is for us too and if we will embrace it and become better rather than bitter.

If we want to unlock resilience, it starts with realizing that God has a plan and then looking forward to what He is going to do in us and through us. The way you are suffering right now? *That's the hard stuff God doesn't want you to waste.*

So what's it look like for you? Maybe it's issues with your family. Maybe you or someone you love is suffering huge health problems. Maybe you carry a broken heart because of the bad decisions made by someone else or by yourself. Maybe you've lost your job. Whatever your suffering, the finished work of Jesus and the presence of the Holy Spirit in your life mean that suffering is not purposeless or random. There is a hope that can change everything, and we're going to start looking for it in the eighth chapter of Romans.[6]

AN INCONVENIENT (BUT OBVIOUS) TRUTH

Let's jump right in, because this good news can't wait. In Romans 8:18, the apostle Paul says, "I consider that the sufferings of this present time are not worthy to be compared with the glory which shall be revealed in us."

---

[6] I'd love for you to read Romans 8 right now on your own. Why don't you set this book down and pick up your Bible for a minute? We're going to be looking at only some of the verses, but the whole chapter is so powerful. And if you're looking for it in the Bible, just remember that chapter 8 always sits conveniently between chapters 7 and 9.

There are two simple but *super*-important truths for us in that verse:

1. Suffering is not optional.
2. Suffering leads to something.

I hate having to say that. But my job is to share the truths Scripture teaches. I get it—sometimes it's easier to ignore difficult truths. But it doesn't help me or you or anyone else to ignore those truths. And by the way, this isn't even a controversial truth. It's inconvenient, yes, but incredibly obvious, whether you look in the pages of the Bible or the pages of your newspaper. Again, everybody hurts.[7]

Paul is basically saying, "Listen, we're going to suffer here on earth, but there's also a glory that's going to be revealed in us." And when he talks about glory, it's not the kind of glory you get from beating your friends at Monopoly or Spades! No, this glory is on a whole different level. It's something we can only *begin* to imagine in our humanness.

Once he establishes that truth, Paul gets cosmic on us—in a good way! The reason we all suffer, he reminds us, is that *all of creation* was unwillingly subjected to the futility and pain of the Fall. Ever since Adam and Eve sinned, our world has been broken. Plants suffer, animals suffer, people suffer— even our water and air suffer. None of that suffering is optional, and there is no permanent remedy for it on this side of eternity (see Romans 8:20–22).

Okay, I hear you saying, "C'mon, Fusco. That's depress-

---

[7] I can't help but hear that line in the vulnerable voice of Michael Stipe, lead singer from R.E.M.

ing." Remember, though, there's something good coming around the bend. Yes, we're headed to heaven if we put our faith in Jesus, but God is promising something for us in *this* life too. And that's where hope comes in. A few verses later, Paul says this: "Hope that is seen is not hope; for why does one still hope for what he sees? But if we hope for what we do not see, we eagerly wait for it with perseverance" (verses 24–25).

I love that! When I'm holding a carne asada burrito from Muchas Gracias,[8] I don't need to hope for it. I already have it![9] But if I'm hungry and I'm headed home from the airport after a long trip, I *hope* Muchas Gracias is still open, you know?

So here's the deal: We're going to be talking a lot in this book about resilient hope. And part of what makes hope resilient and "gritty" is that it's being generated *in the things we can't see.* True hope is us paying forward the trust that we have in the Lord, *especially* in situations where we don't know how things are going to work out. When we feel out of control. When we are in pain. That's where the eagerness in verse 25 comes from. Our hope motivates us to long for God's provision. We can't *wait* to see how He is going to move.

We understand that we're in the middle of the story and there are more chapters to be written. At some point, our story is going to open up. God is the author, and He is working on things we could never dream up on our own.

---

[8]   Actually, every carne asada burrito I have ever eaten has been delicious. I always say yes to burritos.

[9]   My stomach might argue that this is a bad example.

Right now, if you feel trapped in suffering, it's time to start walking in hope. Fix your eyes on the Lord, not on your situation. Looking at only the situation will drive you crazy. But fixing your eyes on Jesus means directing your attention to Him. Rather than just seeing the issues, see Jesus as the solution. Remember that He has a purpose and a plan in the very real and present issues. But don't just give Jesus your attention; choose to trust in His goodness as well.

I admit that isn't the easiest thing to do. I'm still learning it myself. In times of suffering, in times of struggle, in messy situations, I'm learning that I can't just listen to myself. I need to preach to myself, to remind myself to look to Jesus. Whenever I allow my brain to do all the stuff it wants to do, I can start contemplating so many different things that, before I know it, I'm spiraling down. Instead, when I don't know what's going to happen next, I choose hope—and as soon as I do, my mind can start thinking about what God is going to do.

Here's what Paul says earlier, in Romans 5:3–5: "Not only that, but we also glory in tribulations, knowing that tribulation produces perseverance; and perseverance, character; and character, hope. Now hope does not disappoint, because the love of God has been poured out in our hearts by the Holy Spirit who was given to us."

That is such good news! We can praise God in suffering because we know that our tribulations can produce hope. And in our tribulations, God is transforming our character to make us more like Jesus as we move through this world.

Can you see how that kind of hope can make us resilient? Waking up every day, even in suffering, and eagerly anticipating God's creative goodness? This stuff takes patience and perseverance, yes. It takes focusing on a single goal—Jesus—no matter what. It takes pushing everything else to the side.

And for *sure* it takes grit.

But, friends, it's worth it. It's the best investment we could possibly make. And what's amazing is that it pays off for us *and* for others. One of the greatest possible testimonies is when a suffering person walks with unstoppable, resilient hope in God.

A SPIRIT OF HELP

Earlier I told you about my mother's cancer diagnosis and eventual death. Looking back, being with her in her suffering was one of the hardest things I've ever gone through. I know my family would say the same. Sure, it wasn't actually happening to us; it was happening to my mom. But because of our love for her, we suffered alongside her.

Yet in a lot of ways, my mom's passing caused me to ask questions about eternity. Not every twenty-year-old is forced by loss to grapple with thinking about life, death, and eternal life. I'm not saying I wanted to go through all that. I wish my mom wouldn't have had to suffer. I wish she were alive right now. I wish she could have met my bride and our kids and my sisters' spouses and all their kids. How *beautiful* would it be for her to see all that God has done in our lives!

But that isn't what happened. *She* suffered, *we* suffered, and somehow, in the midst of all that not-at-all-optional suffering, hope reared its head.

Living through my mother's suffering and death, and looking back on it twenty years later, gives me confidence and real, daily hope. There was redemption that came through that pain. Since I already know God has done amazing things in the mess of life, I know He will continue to do amazing things. Jesus is as real and present today as ever. So it's my hope that whatever you're going through, whatever suffering is happening in your life right now, you would look to Jesus in the midst of that and walk with Him in unstoppable hope.

What if you could pray a prayer like this?

> *God, I know You're going to do the work. I don't know how You're going to move or when, but whatever happens, I know You're going to work this stuff out in my life.*

Now, I know you might be thinking, *That all sounds a little too perfect. I can't imagine how God's going to work with my suffering.*

I hear that. I've felt that. But the reason we can't imagine how God is going to act is that we're people and not God! With people, things are often impossible, but with God, all things are possible. He can—and does—work in the most horrific situations and is able to bring beauty and light out of ugliness and darkness.

Check out Romans 8:26–27: "The Spirit also helps in our weaknesses. For we do not know what we should pray for as we ought, but the Spirit Himself makes intercession for us with groanings which cannot be uttered. Now He who searches the hearts knows what the mind of the Spirit is, because He makes intercession for the saints according to the will of God."

Even while we are suffering, we already have the help that

we need, even if it's not the kind we would choose. Even in our weakness, and maybe especially in our weakness, God's Spirit is our helper. How many of us have felt like we were missing the words to pray? Like we're suffering so much that we can't get a single word out to God? This passage teaches us that God's Spirit intercedes on our behalf, praying for us when we can't pray on our own.

This is powerful stuff. If you've put your faith and trust in Jesus, the third person of the Trinity has taken up residence in your life.

Jesus called the Spirit "the Helper" (John 14:26), yet how often do we forget that we already have the help we need? The Helper is with you wherever you are today. You only need to ask and lean in.

ALL THINGS?

There's one verse in the eighth chapter of Romans that gets more airtime than all the other verses put together:[10] "We know that all things work together for good" (verse 28).

Sound familiar? If this was anything but the Bible, I might roll my eyes.[11] It sounds like a cliché or something too good to be true. If I told a suffering friend this on my own authority alone, I'd sound pretty out of touch. How can I, an extremely limited[12] human, know for sure that all things work

---

[10]   It's also the verse most likely to be cross-stitched on a pillow at your auntie's house.

[11]   Speaking of eye-rolling, my teenage daughter, Maranatha, might be the world's best eye-roller!

[12]   And extremely hairy.

together for good? I can't—but I don't have to! God's the One who can know that and, more important, the One who can make that happen.

So let's see what the rest of the passage has to say in the midst of our suffering:

> We know that all things work together for good to those who love God, to those who are the called according to His purpose. For whom He fore- knew, He also predestined to be conformed to the image of His Son, that He might be the firstborn among many brethren. Moreover whom He pre- destined, these He also called; whom He called, these He also justified; and whom He justified, these He also glorified. (verses 28–30)

So, basically, God's goal is for us to grow in Jesuslikeness.

I realize that I may have made up that word, *Jesuslikeness,* but I like it, because it's so clear that God's ultimate goal in our suffering is to make us more like His Son. If we open our hearts during seasons of suffering instead of allowing them to harden, God promises to transform us into people who act and speak more like Jesus.[13] So God accomplishes His ultimate transformational work in our lives through our suf- fering. And how refreshing it is to realize our suffering is not for nothing. God is accomplishing something amazing in us!

Growing in Jesuslikeness—including suffering—is how *all* things can work together for good for those who love

---

13 Someone who, by the way, knew a few things about suffering.

God. Now, I'm not going to get into the topic of predestination here, but look at what Paul is showing us about the way God works. There's a process, an order to our lives in Jesus. Ultimately, God leverages whatever trials and tribulations we experience to make us more like Jesus.

And, believe me, it's fine not to enjoy the process! The Bible is overflowing with godly people complaining to God about suffering. But what if we prayed something like this?

> *God, I do not enjoy this. I do not like this one bit.*
> *I do not want this. This hurts. This is breaking my*
> *heart. But, God, make me more like Jesus. I want*
> *You to accomplish Your purposes and plans in me.*

That is where God will meet us. It's where He can change us.

Look, hard things will happen whether we like it or not. Suffering isn't optional. So what's better: suffering for no reason or suffering for a purpose? God doesn't want us to waste our pain, but He won't force us to grow.

All too often, we find ourselves kicking and screaming through the tough times in our lives. But God is there, waiting for us to reach out and grab His hand so we can walk together through the process. We can't afford to waste the hard things. God wants to show us something beautiful.

VICTORY ASSURED

Let's close this chapter with some powerful encouragement.

Read what Paul writes at the end of Romans 8. (I know it's a whole paragraph, but seriously, take a minute to read it.)

What then shall we say to these things? If God is for us, who can be against us? He who did not spare His own son, but delivered Him up for us all, how shall He not with Him also freely give us all things? Who shall bring a charge against God's elect? It is God who justifies. Who is he who condemns? It is Christ who died, and furthermore is also risen, who is even at the right hand of God, who also makes intercession for us. Who shall separate us from the love of Christ? Shall tribulation, or distress, or persecution, or famine, or nakedness, or peril, or sword? As it is written:

> "For Your sake we are killed all day long;
> We are accounted as sheep for the slaughter."

Yet in all these things we are more than conquerors through Him who loved us. For I am persuaded that neither death nor life, nor angels nor principalities nor powers, nor things present nor things to come, nor height nor depth, nor any other created thing, shall be able to separate us from the love of God which is in Christ Jesus our Lord. (verses 31–39)

Our victory is *assured*.

Guaranteed.

And there is *nothing* in the universe that can separate us from the love of God.

It might feel like it sometimes, but you are *never* separated from God's love. A pastor friend of mine once said, "Daniel, the biggest thing we need to learn is not that we need to love God more; it's to learn to let God love us."[14]

See, God loves us more than we can imagine! That means that we are more than conquerors. The game isn't on the line. Life isn't going to come down to some last-second shot where if we miss, we lose. We've already won! Christ has already defeated Satan.

And it's not a super-close victory either. In Jesus, it's a total blowout, a lopsided win. Jesus has run the table. The journey is hard, but the outcome is assured!

Sin and shame are defeated.

Death is conquered.

The tomb is empty.

Creation and hope are restored.

And the Resurrection reigns.

So even though suffering is not optional in this life, we have all the help we need. The Spirit of God is with us. Through all of life, God's ultimate goal is that you and I become more like Jesus. And the more we become like Him, the sweeter life becomes.

That's why the promise of Jesus in John 16:33 is so powerful: "These things I have spoken to you, that in Me you may have peace. In the world you will have tribulation; but be of good cheer, I have overcome the world." Jesus *has* overcome the world. We *can* have peace in Him in the midst of suffering.

---

[14] Thank you immensely to Pastor Rick Warren for our conversation containing this powerful truth.

We're being offered a chance to walk in unstoppable hope. Let's continue the journey together.

> *Father, thank You for helping us see that although suffering is not optional, it is purposeful. We admit that we do not like it, but we see its transformational work in our hearts. Keep our hearts soft and open. Make us more like Jesus.*
>
> *In Jesus's name, amen.*

Unlocking Resilience

1. Author Mika Edmondson has said, "If we won't tell the truth about earthly things people can see, how can they trust us to tell the truth about heavenly things they can't see?"[15] Does this quote make you reconsider the way you talk or think about suffering?

2. What area of suffering has caused you to lose hope? How can you allow Jesus to transform you in that suffering?

3. Buy a dry-erase marker and write a verse from Romans 8 on your bathroom mirror. Memorize it. It really is that important.

4. How does the truth that victory is assured transform our views on what we are suffering?

---

[15] Mika Edmondson (@mika_edmondson), Twitter, January 12, 2021, 11:50 A.M., https://twitter.com/mika_edmondson/status/1349066359339102210.

4

HOPE UNDER PRESSURE
THE BOOK OF JOB

Suffering is a painful part of life. But in suffering, we can come face-to-face with what we really believe about who God is and how He works. Few stories depict this reality more powerfully than the story of Job. Even in the midst of tremendous suffering, even abandoned by family and friends, Job walked in unstoppable hope and gritty faith, and we can do the same.

Early in my walk with Jesus, whistling transformed me.

I know what you're thinking: *Whistling?* But seriously, God put my first mentor in my life because of whistling! I was worshipping in church one day, when I noticed someone whistling the melody to the praise song. As a musician, I've always loved music, and when someone is musically gifted, I can't help but notice. That day, the praise band was rocking, but I was captivated by the sound of the whistling. At first, I wasn't sure what it was. But after looking around without *looking* like I was looking around, I figured out it was this short, thin guy with long white hair, wearing a red sweater, two rows in front of me. When the service ended, I introduced myself. "Man, you've got a beautiful whistle!"[1]

"Well, it's a gift from God, and I'm grateful that I get to use it." His eyes shone and he gave me a huge smile.

His name was Philip. As we became friends,[2] he told me more of his story. He grew up in a family that was completely broken, and he'd suffered from all kinds of health issues his entire life. It seemed like every time he told me something matter-of-fact about his life, it contained so many levels of sadness and pain that it blew my mind.

But what I also noticed (and what was so beautiful) was the quality of his faith. Throughout all the darkness and suffering, there was a bright line of joy and hope, and you could always see it.[3] (Or *hear* it—don't forget his weekly whistling!)

Over the years, I worshipped with Philip more times than I can count. I also visited him in the hospital when he had to go in for one of his frequent surgeries. And he would always say, "No matter how this surgery goes, I know that Jesus

---

[1]   That's an introduction I've used only once in my life—at least so far.

[2]   Philip was the first person who told me I would be a pastor one day. We were standing next to my van, and he noticed it was full of music gear (since I was heading over to a gig). He told me that I should quit music and be a pastor. I thought he was nuts! I gave him a hug and jumped into the van and drove off. We rocked that show. But years later, when I told Philip I was ordained, he just smiled and walked away whistling.

[3]   Philip would share stories that were so heartbreaking that I realized how blessed I was to be raised in my family. This man's journey was almost unbelievable.

loves me and He'll never stop loving me. The Lord is good, and I know someday I'm going to get to see Him."

Philip was filled with more hope than almost anyone I've ever known. He taught me more about God's love than just about anyone else had. Despite the failings he experienced with his own physical father, he showed me how God's love can transform a person into an incredible man of God.

And as I think about Philip, I realize that in each of our lives, hope happens in a context: our context. We don't hope abstractly or in a vacuum. Hope always happens in the context of a particular time and place and a particular life, right? That's why the book of Job is such a wild read.[4] Because of his context.

You'll notice at the top of this chapter that it says we're going to look at Job. Not just a few verses or a chapter, but the entire book. All 42 chapters and 1,070 verses. So I'm not going to quote too many of the verses. In later chapters, you'll get to read an entire short psalm, for example. But in this chapter, we're going to have to deal with some summary—or else you'd be holding a four-hundred-page book! So up front I want to give you an overview of Job. Here's the story in about three hundred words.

Job lived in the land of Uz. He "was blameless and upright, and one who feared God and shunned evil" (Job 1:1). He had a big family and a *way* bigger ranch—so big that he was one of the wealthiest guys in the land. Job was a blessed man. He had it all. He loved his family, and they all enjoyed

---

[4] If you take the time to read the book of Job on your own, I'll award you some bonus Jesus points!

spending time together. Even more important, Job spent time in prayer with God each day. He was faithful. He was rich. He experienced God's gifts.

Then Satan enters the picture. In the story, God and Satan get into a heavenly argument about Job. Satan says that the only reason Job trusts God is that God blesses him and protects him. He tells God that once all Job's blessings are taken away, "he will surely curse You to Your face" (verse 11). Then God gives Satan permission to ruin Job's life—as long as he doesn't actually *take* Job's life. Anything else is fair game, though. This is a bet Satan can't lose. He's sure Job will turn his back on God. But God is sure that Job will remain faithful.[5]

What happens next is tragic. Job loses his children, his wealth, and his health. Job's wife bails on him as well and, in her own grief, tells Job to "curse God and die!" (2:9).

Job's friends arrive, and they spend a few dozen chapters debating extremely heavy stuff—suffering, evil, forgiveness, providence, and so on—but they don't come up with too many answers or insights.

Then, at the climax of the story, God appears in a whirlwind and tells Job and his friends what's really up: God is God, and Job is not! Job remains faithful, and in the years that follow, everything Job had—and much more—is restored to him. The end.[6]

You can probably see why the book of Job is a great place

---

[5] Now, I realize that this opens up a huge can of theological worms. There is so much we can explore in Job. But we won't be unpacking the "How could God agree to this?" question right now.

[6] I had to write that last part because this sounded like a book report!

to go for wisdom about suffering. It is a tremendous example of the "hope + grit" formula at work. All of us suffer, and all of us want to figure out how to make it through to the other side. We want to know how to have hope and hold on when things seem to be at their worst.

YOU'LL BE FAILED, BUT NOT BY GOD

I told you about how I visited my friend Philip in the hospital. He wasn't alone in his suffering, because he had friends like me as well as his faithful wife, Susan. And there's a really cool scene in Job 2 that reminds me of that. Job has three close friends, and like many of our relationships these days, they are scattered in different places. But distance doesn't keep them apart. When Job's three friends hear about all the afflictions that Job experienced, they make a plan to visit him. Doesn't that feel so contemporary? Like when college friends plan a reunion weekend or when you fly across the country to be with a close friend who is going through a divorce or living with terminal cancer?

So Job's three friends—Eliphaz the Temanite, Bildad the Shuhite, and Zophar the Naamathite, to be exact[7]—roll up to Job's place, and they can't believe their eyes. Job's estate is a wreck, and Job himself is a wreck—so much so that the friends don't even recognize him at first. Then, in solidarity with Job's suffering, the friends rip their robes, sprinkle dust on their heads, and weep (see verses 11–12). Check out what happens next:

---

[7]   Hearing their names makes me think I should go by Daniel the Fuscoite from now on. Thoughts?

> They sat down with him on the ground seven days
> and seven nights, and no one spoke a word to
> him, for they saw that his grief was very great.
> (verse 13)

How often do we make space like that in times of suffering? What a gift they gave Job. After all, what was there to be said? This is an important lesson about how to sit with people who are suffering. Pastor Rick Warren has said, "When people are in deep pain they don't need explanations, advice, encouragement, or even Scripture. They just need you to show up and shut up."[8] It may sound terse, but Pastor Rick was dropping some serious wisdom by reminding us that people need our presence more than they need our platitudes. We may not want to add any more pain or sorrow, but we can find ourselves saying "helpful" things that are actually the opposite.

Now prepare for some whiplash. Ready? I know that I *just* talked about how great Job's friends were. But the book of Job has quite a few more chapters, and pretty soon things get real ugly, real quick! In a nutshell, once the weeklong moment of silence is over, Job's friends get into a *long* discussion with him about his suffering, and one point gets hammered home: Somehow it must be Job's fault.

Job's friends can't imagine that he is innocent or faithful. They figure that if he were, none of the bad stuff would have happened to him. So rather than comforting Job in his dis-

---

[8]   Rick Warren (@RickWarren), Twitter, July 13, 2018, 5:57 P.M., https://twitter.com/rickwarren/status/1017920895220772864.

tress, his friends begin to make his pain even worse. Instead of mourning, Job is forced to argue and defend himself.[9]

It's unfortunate, but it's true: In times of great suffering, our friends and our family can fail us. All too often, the people who are closest to us, the people who are supposed to be there for us, fail to help us.

One thing that may ease that ache, at least for followers of Jesus, is to remember that our Lord had that exact same experience. I mean, think about Matthew 26:33, where Peter brags that no matter what everyone else does, he will *never* reject Jesus. And Jesus sees right through him and is like, "Really, Peter? You're going to deny Me three times before the night is over" (see verse 34).

In the next verse, Peter of course swears he'd rather die with Jesus than deny Him, but he denies Him all the same. Or think about that same night, when Jesus wants to pray with his three closest friends in the Garden of Gethsemane. And instead of keeping watch with Jesus and supporting Him, they fall asleep (see verses 36–40)! He's literally sweating drops of blood as He prays, and they're snoring in the bushes.[10]

And the rejections kept right on happening. Most of the public was turning their backs on the one they'd welcomed and praised only a week earlier. Even as Jesus was dying, He cried out with a loud voice, "My God, My God, why have You forsaken Me?" (27:46).

---

[9]   This happens today just like it did back then.

[10]   Now, the Bible doesn't say that they were actually snoring. But it is still within the realm of possibility.

Listen, rejection in the face of suffering happened to Job, it happened to Jesus, and, unfortunately, it's going to happen to us. I'm not saying that it *should* happen. It shouldn't. But it does. We'll face times when our closest friends, our closest family members won't be at our sides when we need them most. I don't know about you, but sometimes for me that rejection feels even worse than the suffering!

But here's the flip side: Jesus is faithful, even when no one else is. God can—and does—comfort us during suffering. I can't even guess how many times I've quoted the following passage in my role as a pastor:

> Blessed be the God and Father of our Lord Jesus Christ, the Father of mercies and God of all comfort, who comforts us in all our tribulation, that we may be able to comfort those who are in any trouble, with the comfort with which we ourselves are comforted by God. For as the sufferings of Christ abound in us, so our consolation also abounds through Christ. Now if we are afflicted, it is for your consolation and salvation, which is effective for enduring the same sufferings which we also suffer. Or if we are comforted, it is for your consolation and salvation. And our hope for you is steadfast, because we know that as you are partakers of the sufferings, so also you will partake of the consolation." (2 Corinthians 1:3–7)

That is such a good message for us. I think this passage comes up so often because whatever trials we go through, everyone needs a reminder that comfort is possible and that it has to begin with the "God of all comfort." It's as though God is a well that never runs out of water, and every person can drink from it.

COMFORTED TO BE A COMFORT

God is relentlessly relational. The gifts He gives us are very rarely just for ourselves. In our suffering, in the pressure cooker of life, whatever comfort we receive from God is always meant for a dual purpose. Yes, He comforts us. And then we are meant to share that comfort with others who are going through something similar. In business terms, it's as if He leverages each single experience of suffering to help many other people.

Friends, every time one of God's kids suffers, a testimony is created—a story of God's redemption and faithfulness and grace.

In my life there are so many painful experiences that God has turned into testimonies—into ways I can bless others. Whether it's addiction or grief or disappointment, I can speak hope to people going through similar things *because* I suffered too. Recently, I sat with a young man who was struggling to stay consistent on his journey with Jesus. The world around him was filled with temptations, and he had developed a habit of not only giving in to them but also putting himself in situations where he would be vulnerable. I knew this pattern well because it was part of my story. We all need to start our journeys with Jesus by unlearning certain things. And if I hadn't suffered and failed earlier in my life, I wouldn't have been able to bring a bit of God's peace to this young man.

The local church is one of the main places where this sharing of experiences happens.[11] In many ways, God's people are at their best when life is at its worst. The body of Christ can rally around somebody in the most horrific situation. Broken but redeemed people helping other broken people is so beautiful to witness and be part of. When we're suffering, God wants us to receive from other people the comfort that they've received.

Here's another way of looking at it: Will you suffer? Will those you know suffer? Unfortunately, yes. It's inevitable.

So don't waste the hard things.

My friends, God can use suffering to grow us up and mature us. Think about it: Everyone suffers in life! It's one of the only universals in this fallen world. But our suffering can either make us bitter or make us better. Becoming bitter wastes the hard things. What a waste it would be if suffering were pointless or irredeemable. Some people talk about suffering as if it's the worst thing in the world—like it proves God is out of control or can't be trusted. But that's true only if suffering is random and senseless.

James puts this spin on it:

> My brethren, count it all joy when you fall into various trials, knowing that the testing of your faith produces patience. But let patience have its perfect work, that you may be perfect and complete, lacking nothing. If any of you lacks wisdom, let him ask of God, who gives to all liberally

---

[11] I never want to miss an opportunity to remind you about how much we need the church. And the church needs us too.

and without reproach, and it will be given to him.
(James 1:2–5)

I love that, especially when I read it as more an invitation than a command. I *can* count it joy when various trials slap me around. I won't always be perfect, but it's what I should be aiming for. Why? So some more sweet fruit of the Spirit[12] can grow in my life! In this case, the fruit is patience, and I don't know about you, but I could always use more of that.[13]

And I love the second part of what James says as well: If we lack wisdom, all we must do is ask God for some. And He doesn't say, "Oh, you need *My* wisdom? Typical. Fine, here's some wisdom . . . I guess." That's not who God is. Our Father is so generous! He doesn't give us a hard time just because we need something like more wisdom. It's the opposite: He gives us tons of it, gladly.

Have you ever felt at a loss for how to comfort someone? Have you ever felt awkward or fearful around suffering? Just ask God for help! The God of all comfort can comfort you, and He will give you the wisdom to bring comfort to someone else.

HOPE RISES

You might be thinking, *Fusco, you had one Job, er . . . one job in this chapter about the book of Job, and that was to*

---

[12] Can you can name the other eight fruits? If you need help, check out Galatians 5:22–23. And don't miss my book *Crazy Happy: Nine Surprising Ways to Live the Truly Beautiful Life*. We dig in and explore the fruit of the Spirit and unpack some amazing stuff!

[13] To be honest, I may be the least patient person I have ever met.

talk about Job! So let's get back to him. Thanks for the encouragement. Okay.

When suffering hits us, friends and family might fail us. That's not what is meant to happen. God's plan is for us to dwell in Him and His comfort and provision[14] and then go out into our families and communities and love and comfort others. To paraphrase Scripture, we love others because we are loved by God (see 1 John 4:11).

But sometimes we find ourselves truly alone. God never deserts us, of course, yet everyone else might. How do we respond in situations like that? How do we hang on to hope when everything seems hopeless?

I want to suggest something that might sound a little funny at first, so bear with me. I don't have a neat five-step plan for hanging on to hope, but I *do* have the example of Job, and it's wild. Here's what he says in chapter 19, right in the thick of his way-too-long dialogue with his friends, who have sadly become his frenemies.

> Oh, that my words were written!
> Oh, that they were inscribed in a book!
> That they were engraved on a rock
> With an iron pen and lead, forever!
> For I know that my Redeemer lives,
> And He shall stand at last on the earth;
> And after my skin is destroyed, this I know,
> That in my flesh I shall see God,
> Whom I shall see for myself,

---

[14] Skip ahead to chapter 13 if you want to read more about this.

And my eyes shall behold, and not another.
How my heart yearns within me! (verses 23–27)

Brothers and sisters, that is straight *fire* from Brother Job!
He's so confident in what he's saying that he wants his words
written down. No, scratch that—he wants them published in
a book![15]

Actually, books can be destroyed. He wants his words
commemorated for all time, carved into a rock.[16] Job is like,
"I will go to my grave knowing just a few things with certainty. God, my Redeemer, lives. He's coming back. And
when I die, I'll be united with God."

That's the gospel, way back in the book of Job! This is so
awesome, because in the garden of suffering, there is a well-
spring of hope. Even though Job's lost all his material pos-
sessions, his soul is still emboldened by the reality that his
God is a redeemer. All hope is not lost. Sure, the situation is
bleak, but Job won't give up.

And then there's this incredible line at the end: "How my
heart yearns within me!"

That's haunting. That's the hope that fuels Job's life.
Speaking what will happen in the future motivates Job in
the present. He *cannot wait* to see God. Nothing painful in
his life compares to the hope he has. Not losing family
members. Not losing money and status and health. His suffering is awful, yes. He admits that for sure. But still, burn-
ing at his core is a hope that no suffering can quench. And

---

[15] I can relate.

[16] Can we can get this book inscribed on a rock? Pretty please?

his hopeful mindset feeds his gritty ability, despite all obstacles.

Now, you may be wondering how Job can be so certain of this. How can he hang on when everything around him seems to argue that he should let go?

Well, here's the crazy part.

Job is . . . just certain! He was certain before calamity struck, and he still is afterward. Nothing his friends have said has swayed him one way or the other. The hope that explodes out of Job in verses 23–27 didn't come out of nowhere; it came from what he already knew about God. And this hope fueled Job's gritty determination. Job was still there, trusting God and waiting on Him to move.

Now, you might be saying, "Fusco, thanks for this. Job may have had certainty, but I'm not Job. And I'm in the worst way possible."

If that is you, first let me say that I am totally sorry. For all of it. But here's the thing: What if, as He did with Job, God wants to cultivate the certainty that will make your life unstoppable? What if this present suffering is actually a miraculous gift in disguise? What if you will look back on this grueling chapter in your life and say, "I grew more through that suffering than at any other point in my life"?

My friends, never forget that trusting Jesus is a choice. So *make* that choice, and hold on for dear life.

It begins with a decision of the mind, but it doesn't stop there. Once you have made the choice, you must let that mental assent permeate your will and emotions. It's not just a mind game. It changes our feelings and motivations. And then, ultimately, you put feet on your trust in Jesus as you walk forward with a hopeful resilience and confidence.

Like a diamond, hope is created under pressure. Like gold, hope is refined in the fire. But that fire is pain. In some ways, Job is a human definition of grit. He represents resilience. Job's journey was challenging. He rarely understood what God was doing. He also couldn't fathom why bad things were happening. Job often sounded completely hopeless. Yet no circumstance in his life, however painful, was stronger than his decision to trust God and *keep on* trusting Him, especially when he didn't understand the purpose of it all. If he can lose everything and yet praise God, we have an example we can follow. There is a hard sort of comfort in that, isn't there?

Remember that Jesus is real. Our suffering is real too. I know that. Not better than anyone, but I certainly know that. Yet our suffering is not forever. It literally can't be forever! Only Jesus is real *and* forever.

Think of that hope that animated Job, even while his body was covered in painful sores and he sat in the ashes of his former life. What would a rising hope look like in your life? In the midst of your struggles and suffering, what would it look like for you to cry out that your Redeemer lives? That Jesus loves you the same yesterday, today, and forever? When Jesus comes back, He's going to do something so mind blowing that I want you to read it on a single line.

Jesus is going to set right everything that is wrong.

To quote the meaning of the name of my daughter *Maranatha*, "O Lord, come!"[17]

When we understand that the coming of Jesus means the end of every tear—think about that, the end of every single

---

[17] 1 Corinthians 16:22.

reason to weep—we can't help but join with Job in hope. In fact, our Bibles are full of stories of people who suffered intensely and still had hope rise within them. Elijah. Jeremiah. David. Esther. Stephen. And I could list dozens more, because the story of God's people is the story of hope rising under pressure.

For I know that my Redeemer lives! And not just lives, but loves and saves.

GOD IS GOD, AND WE ARE NOT

Job is a strange and confusing book. But even for a strange book, it ends . . . strangely.

Remember I told you that Job and his friends have a polite chat about what seems like some pretty unimportant stuff (ahem) for dozens of chapters? You might expect the end of Job's story to have, well, an end. But what really happens is that someone new enters the chat:

> Then the LORD answered Job out of the whirlwind.
>   (38:1)

And guess what? For the next several chapters, God is asking Job questions and not answering Job's questions! It's kind of crazy. *God never answers Job's deepest question.* God never says, "Here's why all this happened, Job." Instead, after pages and pages and *pages* of discussions and accusations and questions between all the humans involved in Job's life, God shows up and basically tells Job to stop talking and *listen.*

And here's a dangerously short summary of what God says.

God is God.

Job is a human.

End of story.

Well, almost the end.

Ultimately, the story of Job ends with God restoring Job's health and livelihood. Job also got to have more children. Now, don't get me wrong—these later-in-life blessings do not heal the pain of the suffering that Job endured. But we do see the goodness of God at the end of the story in Job's life. God is a God of redemption and restoration.

One of the greatest gifts we can receive in our times of suffering is to remember that *we can trust God, even if He doesn't explain Himself to us.* It's true and difficult at the same time.

That doesn't mean God doesn't answer *any* questions. I know God's answered plenty of my own over the years— sometimes right away and sometimes further down the road. But I also know I've asked some pretty urgent questions that *didn't* get answered, or at least haven't been yet.[18]

For me, part of this comes down to choosing to walk by faith. Scripture says that "we walk by faith, not by sight" (2 Corinthians 5:7). Scripture also says that the ways of God are not the ways of humanity (see Isaiah 55:8–9). If God told me everything—assuming my tiny little brain and heart could process what I was being told—then I wouldn't have to trust God at all. I would know everything and could choose to obey or not. But that's not the way God designed it to

---

[18] I like to tell people that I have a filing cabinet of questions that I can't wait to ask the Lord when I get to heaven. But then I remind people that when I get to heaven, I probably won't be worried about any of that stuff!

work. And He is uniquely pleased when we choose to walk by faith, trusting Him with childlike faith.

Whether or not God answers a particular question of ours doesn't change His trustworthiness.

Stop for a moment. Don't miss that.

Here it is in another way: God is trustworthy even if He doesn't answer all our questions.

If you're a parent, think of how you don't answer all your kid's questions. Sometimes that's because he or she asks what seems like an infinite number of them! But other times you have a wise reason for not answering or for answering in a certain way or at a certain time. You know more than your child.[19]

Getting back to Job, we see something very powerful about trust. In Job 13:15, in the midst of all his suffering, Job says the following about God: "Though He slay me, yet will I trust Him."

That's almost an insane thing to say!

It's also powerful. In your suffering, what Satan wants is to tell you, "God doesn't love you. You can't trust God. God's got ill intentions toward you." And he wants to steal, kill, and destroy the relationship that God bought for you on Calvary's cross (see John 10:10). The Enemy wants us to expect God to explain. Every. Single. Thing.

But God doesn't need to explain anything to anyone, as we see in the book of Job. Why not? Because God is God! We aren't God's equals. We just aren't. God actually doesn't owe us an explanation about anything. We can be like, "God, I *demand* You tell me everything!" and God can be like, "Nope."

---

[19] I hope.

There's an amazing section of the book of Hebrews I want to share with you:

> We also, since we are surrounded by so great a cloud of witnesses, let us lay aside every weight, and the sin which so easily ensnares us, and let us run with endurance the race that is set before us, looking unto Jesus, the author and finisher of our faith, who for the joy that was set before Him endured the cross, despising the shame, and has sat down at the right hand of the throne of God. (12:1–2)

Like Job—one of our great cloud of witnesses—we need to keep our eyes on the ultimate goal. What is God's plan for you *and* for all humanity? That Jesus would willingly choose to experience shame and endure the cross. Why? So that through His perfect life, death, and resurrection, sin and death would be conquered. That's the ultimate goal. Jesus didn't just point the way; He blazed the trail with His own life and death. And because of His selfless work on the cross for us, we run our races with perseverance and endurance. We keep on going . . . in Jesus's name.

Suffering has the ability to be an extraordinary teacher. That's absolutely true. But please hear my heart on this. None of us want to suffer. None of us look forward to it. And suffering totally sucks.[20] I would never want to trivialize someone's pain. We know suffering will happen. It just will.

---

[20] I realize that this choice of word is provocative, but it is honest. If it's offensive to you, please forgive me.

So maybe we could say, "Lord, I'm suffering. I know I'll suffer more. Would You revolutionize my outlook? I want to run this race to win the prize. Let me run with endurance and let me look to You, knowing that You went through hard things, but God was doing a great work, and You're doing a work in my life right now."

Whatever you're going through right now—and I truly mean whatever—God knows everything about it. And not just in some factual, intellectual way either. It's much more personal than that. God knows the intimate facts of your situation, yes, but His knowledge and involvement don't stop there. He created you, loves you, and watches over you. And because He knows suffering will happen in this fallen world and in your life in particular, He wants to comfort you. And He wants hope to rise up within your suffering.

God wants to do a work in and through the sufferings that we endure with grit and determination. And He asks us to trust Him. When we do that, we live—like our brother Job— with a resilient, unstoppable hope. And not only during whatever we're going through right now but in anything we might experience in the future.

Unlocking Resilience

1. In what areas are you struggling with the sufferings you experience? Is there subtle suffering that you are enduring?

2. Read the scene in Job 2 where Job's wife cries out, "Do you still hold fast to your integrity? Curse God and die!" (verse 9). How does Job answer?

3. Choose to be present for a suffering friend. And try to stay silent and just be there.

4. What would ruthless trust look like?

5

THE CONTEXT FOR RENEWAL

ISAIAH 40:31

God is in the business of making all things new. He wants this newness to be present in every part of our lives. But how does renewal happen? Renewal happens when, in the context of our present lives, we move upward, inward, and outward with God.

"If you want to make God laugh, start making plans."

You've heard something like that before, right?[1] It's funny, but the idea behind it comes straight out of Scripture (see James 4:13–14). Now, I don't really think God is sitting around waiting for us to make plans just so He can laugh at us, but it's undeniably true that His purposes and plans are different from ours. No matter how much planning we do

---

[1] This is actually an old Yiddish proverb: *Mann tracht und Gott lacht.* Which roughly translated says, "Men plan and God laughs."

and no matter how wonderful those plans are, God often has something completely different in mind for us. And usually what God has in mind for us is *renewal*.

This view about making plans brings back memories of my own journey as a musician. From the first time I saw a rock band playing on TV, I knew I wanted to be a rock star. There was just something about those guys up on stage, rocking out in a stadium packed with cheering fans!

But how could I get there? Being the all-around genius that I was,[2] I decided that learning how to play an instrument might be a good first step. So I picked up the bass guitar in middle school, and—presto!—I was quickly offered a spot in a few different bands. My plan was off to a fantastic start!

When it came time for the high school Battle of the Bands, I was more than ready.[3] I didn't know if I'd be hated or cele-brated, but it was time to find out. The whole experience turned out to be amazing. Standing up on stage, with so many people watching, made all the practice and hard work worthwhile. Though, to be honest, I stood frozen in one spot, barely moving and hoping I wouldn't hit any wrong notes. I'd have to work on my rock-star persona, but at least I grinned for all I was worth!

As I progressed through high school and college, my skill level on the bass guitar steadily improved. I decided to branch out and learn the upright bass, which brought me a whole new set of challenges. But I didn't shy away from them. And as I kept practicing my instrument and playing with better

---

[2]   Said with my tongue firmly planted in my cheek.

[3]   This moment was even bigger because I was still in middle school playing at the high school.

and better bands, I realized that I wanted to pursue music as a career after college. I'm pretty sure my parents weren't thrilled about my employment prospects, but I sure was.

Now, please don't judge me, but at certain times, I did find myself posing in front of a mirror with my bass guitar, practicing for the cover shot for a future *Bass Player* magazine feature article. I couldn't wait to grace their cover with my long dreadlocks, dashing good looks, and monstrous bass licks!

So here's the question: Do you think that ever happened?

Sure, I had plans—and they seemed like pretty good ones too!—but God laughed. He had completely different plans that I couldn't even begin to imagine! (How could I imagine becoming a pastor when I didn't even know Jesus?)

See, it wasn't that my plans were bad. All things considered, they were relatively harmless. But God wanted to renew my life, and my plans had nothing to do with that. When God called me to follow Him, He knew my life needed to go in a new direction. And as He started to do His work of renewal in my life, my music took a back seat to His plans.

Renewal is growth through change—growth directed and empowered by God's Spirit working in the world and in our hearts. This growth happens only as we continue on with resilience. God's plan of renewal is the fruit on the other side of showing up for life with all its messes. Growth takes place over time. And resilience allows us to stay engaged in the process.

We plan where a relationship is headed, and God plans renewal. We plan to transfer to a new job, and God plans renewal. We plan renewal, and God plans *God's* kind of renewal.

That might sound scary, especially when you're comfortable with the way things are. I don't know about you, but I enjoy knowing (or thinking I know) what's going to happen next week and next month and next year. But God has been teaching me the beauty in this kind of change of plans. He knew that we would be right here, right now, during a unique season.

Many of our churches had big plans for 2020. I can remember how excited I was for our church family to make a huge impact, but that excitement soon turned from disappointment to disillusionment as an invisible virus turned all our lives upside down. As our plans evaporated, I had to do some serious soul searching and talking with God to come to terms with what was happening in our community and world. And I've heard this same story more times than I can count. Even as I write this, there are still so many unknowns.

Change like that can be a challenge, but when God renews us, it's always a good thing. Being encouraged and uplifted by His Spirit as we become more like Jesus is always a good thing. But what we need to realize is that the context for our renewal is, well, whatever *our* context is, and God's in control of that!

We sometimes assume that renewal happens in "spiritual" contexts, like when we go to a camp or retreat center or we pray for an hour with a group of prayer warriors. And it can happen in those contexts, for sure. But you don't have to be some super-spiritual person who spends ten hours a day reading the Bible and praying in order for renewal to happen.[4] If that were the case, stay-at-home parents and

---

[4] Although if you do live like this, renewal is inevitable and you are even more likely to see it and respond to it.

microchip designers and commercial fishers could never be renewed.

The truth is, renewal is for all of us. Any life stage, any job, anytime, any*one*.

Look, God isn't scratching His head about any of us. It's not like He's going, "Hmm, I planned to help Liz become more Christlike as she trained for a marathon, but now that the race is canceled, I'm out of options. Sorry, Liz, no renewal for you!"

Maybe you're unemployed right now. Or retired. Or doing online high school. Or wanting to have kids. Or raising kids. Or taking care of aging parents. Guess what? Wherever you are is God's context for your renewal—the context in which He wants you to be discipled. If you're married, God will use your marriage as one of the primary contexts in which to make you more like Jesus. And if you're single? Being single is one of the primary contexts in which Jesus will do a work in your life.

No matter our age or stage or place in life, God wants to do a work in our lives. And that's true in *any* context, even one that is off-the-charts unprecedented and difficult. The only question is, Will we embrace renewal right where we are?

A WORK OF RENEWAL

Saying that God wants to renew us might sound a bit abstract, so I want to give us an image we can hang on to. Fortunately, the prophet Isaiah has a perfect one for us. Let's open the Bible to one of its most famous verses, Isaiah 40:31:

> Those who wait on the LORD
> Shall renew their strength;

They shall mount up with wings like eagles,
They shall run and not be weary,
They shall walk and not faint.

In the rest of this chapter, we're going to see how those images describe both the how and why of renewal God has planned for us. And as a bonus, I'm going to show you that this verse is a perfect, powerful example of a God-breathed system for living that we see repeated in Scripture and in our lives as well: upward, inward, outward.

If you don't have my book *Upward, Inward, Outward: Love God, Love Yourself, Love Others,* you should probably pause reading *this* book and head to your nearest bookstore and treat yourself to a copy. I kid, I kid.[5] But especially as we consider God's renewal in our life, the idea I want to explore here comes straight out of the Greatest Commandment, when Jesus tells us, " 'You shall love the LORD your God with all your heart, with all your soul, and with all your mind.' This is the first and great commandment. And the second is like it: 'You shall love your neighbor as yourself' " (Matthew 22:37–39).

God invites all of us, at all times, to live upward, inward, and outward. At every moment of our lives, it's like God is saying, "Start with your relationship with Me, and My love for you will change the way you see yourself and the way you treat others."

Our Isaiah text shows a very similar upward-inward-outward movement to those well-known words of Jesus.

---

5   Seriously, though, you should read that book. I go so much deeper into this amazing system for living than I can in this chapter.

We're going to see how waiting on the Lord, hoping in the Lord, begins everything. Trusting that God is doing a great work in us, even in uncertain times, is the upward movement that begins everything. It's the launching pad for unstoppable hope and fail-proof faith. Then, as our strength is renewed, we come together, inward, as the church. God is the all-powerful One, and in our weakness, His strength is made perfect. He wants to do a work of renewal in all our hearts. Why? To send us outward—sometimes flying like eagles, sometimes running quickly, and other times managing to grit it out in a slower walk, but still without losing hope.

MOVING UPWARD

Okay, let's start by looking at what I called the launching pad: our intimacy with God, through Jesus. This is the first part of our Isaiah 40:31 image, where we "mount up with wings like eagles." Intimacy is something we all want in our relationships, right? And I'm not just talking about physical intimacy either. I find it sad that intimacy these days almost always refers to only sexuality. I've always thought of intimacy as being more than simply a physical relationship.

Real, lasting, all-in intimacy is the basis of the best and deepest relationships. My favorite definition of intimacy is "communication over time." Researchers tell us that there are numerous types of communication: verbal, nonverbal, written, listening, and visual.[6] The relationships we treasure most tend to be the ones where we've enjoyed the deepest

---

6   Anne Converse Willkomm, "Five Types of Communication," Drexel University, Goodwin College of Professional Studies, July 12, 2018, https://drexel.edu/graduatecollege/professional-development/blog/2018/July/Five-types-of-communication.

communication for the longest time. Think about any relationship you have: It began with communication. Sometimes even in unlikely ways. If we talk to someone enough times, eventually a relationship automatically forms. That doesn't mean we become best friends with everyone we talk to, but it does mean that we can't go deeper if we aren't communicating.

It reminds me of when I first met my wife, Lynn. I thought she was amazing, but there was one problem: We weren't living in the same city. So we talked on the phone quite a bit. Now, keep in mind, back then unlimited cell phone plans weren't a thing.[7] One month, we went so far over her allotted minutes that her cell phone bill came in at seven hundred dollars! (Gulp.) Did it cost a lot? Yes! Was it worth the money? *Absolutely.*

Clearly, then, if we want to grow in our relationships with Jesus, we need communication over time. So how do we grow our communication with Him? Lots of ways! We're all different, and we're all going to have paths we are more or less comfortable on. We can read the Bible. We can pray. We can journal. We can paint or sing. We can talk to God while we're stuck in traffic. We can sit in stillness and increase our awareness of His presence. There are countless ways to reach out and connect with Him.

Remember, we're doing this to launch us upward, toward our Father. "Those who wait on the LORD shall renew their strength" (Isaiah 40:31). And not just that, but "mount up with wings like eagles." Our renewal begins with our up-

---

[7] We are pretty old. Okay, actually I am old, and Lynn is angelically forever young.

ward relationship with God, through Jesus. Our resilience, or grit, is found by tapping into God's strength. It all begins with the upward movement of our relationships with God.

I want to encourage you to learn to simply spend time hanging out with Jesus. Enjoy "wasting your time" on Him![8] Think about your best friend, the one you can do absolutely nothing with and still enjoy every minute. Don't you find yourself built up by the time you spend together? Think about people in your life you can spend time in silence with, just appreciating one another's presence. Aren't those relationships life giving, hope building, and encouraging? What if it was like that with Jesus? What if you invited Him to join you on your next hike or the next time you mow the lawn? When was the last time you spent an entire afternoon hanging out with Him?

That's why I encourage you to read your Bible. That's why I encourage you to journal, even if that looks like talking out loud in your car as you drive home from work. When was the last time you wrote down your fears and hopes and prayers? When was the last time you spent more than a minute thanking God for everything He's done in your life?

These disciplines and the many others like them help us unlock resilience in numerous ways. We have to remember to train before the race. We want to be spiritually in shape and built up before the trials happen. Scripture, gratitude, and journaling help us see life through the lens of God's kingdom. They also make us become more attentive to the flow

---

[8] I am being facetious with the idea of "wasting your time." No time spent with Jesus is ever wasted. And instead of playing video games or streaming another TV show, that's how we should be spending our free time.

of God's Spirit. Our awareness of God's work in the midst of our messy world pays huge dividends in cultivating the resilience that comes with the mind of Christ.

David puts it so well in Psalm 63:1:

> O God, You are my God;
> Early will I seek You;
> My soul thirsts for You;
> My flesh longs for You
> In a dry and thirsty land
> Where there is no water.

Listen, we get to go as deep into relationship with God as we want! There is no limit to the amount He loves us. He is always there for us and wants to spend time with us. It will never happen that we say, "Lord, I want to spend time with You," and He is like, "Nah, I'm too busy for you right now." Every single time we turn to God, He's there.

Here's another beautiful image from Scripture that gives us a sense of how God sees His children. Zephaniah 3:17 blows my mind and fills my heart every time I hear it.[9]

> The LORD your God in your midst,
> The Mighty One, will save;
> He will rejoice over you with gladness,
> He will quiet you with His love,
> He will rejoice over you with singing.

---

[9] Check out the album *Seeds of Praise* by Seeds Family Worship for a killer song version ("Mighty to Save") of this verse!

You can sense that the Father has pulled His children close, as they're desiring to spend time with Him, and He is just flooded with joy. And He will quiet us with His love. There is so much turbulence in our culture, and so much turbulence inside us. We're worried about so many things. Amazing, amazing . . . God even *sings* over us!

When was the last time you were blown away that God loves to spend time with you? He absolutely loves that—so much that He can't keep His love inside and so He sings it forth. When kids grow up and move out of the house, that's often the first time they discover how much they love—and miss—their parents. For many of us, it's been a long time since we came back home to our heavenly Father and said, "Father, I missed You!" And when we do that, we discover that God has been waiting for us all along, ready to rejoice over us.

So know this: You're never alone. *Never.* No matter how isolated you feel, how abandoned you feel, you aren't alone. God is with you. He is in your midst, and He *will* save. That's the hope-filled, upward relationship that our faith is built on, and it leads to something wonderful.

MOVING INWARD

As we trust God, He changes us and grows us to be more like Jesus. When we wait on the Lord, He will meet us where we are and rejoice over us.

For what purpose, though? Well, one reason is for God's own glory. This might be a challenge for some of us, but let's go there for a minute. We give God praise because He is real and personal and will transform us for His own glory. He is beyond amazing. Even when we have made poor choices or experienced adversity in our lives, He faithfully works to renew us.

That's one of the reasons people give God the glory for their success and achievements. For people of faith, they realize that they didn't do the work—God did it in and through them. While those who don't know God might scoff at the notion, people of faith are convinced that He has a greater purpose for them and is doing a work in them. We shouldn't forget the importance of God glorifying Himself by renewing people like us.

The Lord desires to do a unique work of transformation and restoration inside each one of us. This inner work, done by the Spirit because of the finished work of Jesus, is how we overcome all the messes of life. Resilience is formed in us by the Spirit. And we walk, step by step, in hope, through the issues we face. The ability to walk forward is because of God's work inward, in our hearts and souls.

What is powerful is that Jesus makes us the kind of people who walk in resilience and grit. He works these qualities in in us, and ultimately we walk them out in real time. And God is glorified when we walk forward in faith.

Do you know what happens when you take a bunch of people who are being renewed by God and stick them together? You get church.

Now, the whole idea of attending church on Sundays has fallen on hard times. I get that. We live in a highly individualistic culture. We want to go out to eat on Sunday mornings or get some errands done or watch our kids play sports. We don't want someone to tell us we have to change how we spend our time and attention and money. We think life is all about us, and if we want to add spirituality into the mix, we'll figure out our *own* way to do that, thank you very much. We don't need some pastor or priest deciding everything for us, do we?

And at the same time, we live in a culture where new collectives are popping up left and right and old ones are flourishing. People crave community and use things like book clubs and lunch bunches to fill that void. But there is also an increasing push to abandon the idea of being part of the church.

What God shows us in the Bible is that life isn't just about us as individuals—and it isn't about individuals making up their own collective groups either! What life *is* about is individuals—absolutely all of us—being called to be part of something bigger and greater and God-focused: the church.

It might seem a little strange to be talking about church as part of an inward movement. Maybe it is!

But our current cultural moment got me thinking about different ways to understand God's inward movement. You see, looking inward encompasses how we see ourselves and our identities and whether they truly are rooted in Jesus. But then when we zoom out a bit, we can see that all of our transformed lives are moving inward toward the same destination, which is relationship with Jesus and one another.

In my context, that's Crossroads Community Church,[10] but there are millions of churches. Each one is made up of people who experience an upward relationship with God and who are called together, inward, to be part of something

---

[10] Check us out at https://crossroadschurch.net.

bigger.[11] I see this as the middle part of our Isaiah image: Together, we "shall run and not be weary."

God's design for each of us is that we find ourselves part of something bigger. I'm sure you've heard the saying that if you want to go fast, you go alone, but if you want to go far, you go together. In many ways, that describes the church. We come together for several purposes. First and foremost, we gather to worship God. But there's something else the church is uniquely able to do, in ways that isolated individuals cannot.

I want you to hear how the writer of Hebrews puts it: "Let us consider one another in order to stir up love and good works, not forsaking the assembling of ourselves together, as is the manner of some, but exhorting one another, and so much the more as you see the Day approaching" (Hebrews 10:24–25).

This passage is powerful for us.

In recent times, we've learned more than ever that we can't take gathering together for granted. In fact, the ability to gather together physically was taken from many of us, at least for a time. But what happened? We immediately figured out how to keep meeting together, digitally. It was a movement of churches of all sizes and styles across the world. And it was so powerful that it crashed streaming services everywhere! That isn't all the church is meant to be, of course, but by God's grace, we found new ways to not forsake each other.

---

[11] I love how the apostle Paul puts it in Romans 8:28: that God is working "all things . . . together for good to those who love God, to those who are the called according to *His* purpose."

We continued to consider one another in order to stir up love and good works. That can happen on a digital screen, just as it can through a front-porch screen.

Catch this next part: Our Hebrews verse has the words "as is the manner of some" (verse 25). Forget about people who have stopped attending church for a second. How many people are not truly engaged with their church family, even if they attend regularly? Maybe they show up but are not really involved and not serving. They're not living their faith out. Many people are concerned about declining church attendance, but I'm just as concerned with how disengaged many of the regular attenders seem to be. Instead of running together and not growing weary, they're just standing around, individually, going nowhere.

Something the past few years have shown me is that we need to be the church twenty-four hours a day, seven days a week. We shouldn't be financially generous only when we attend a function at church; we should be financially generous because God is the most generous person we've ever met. We shouldn't serve each other only when doing so is organized by our church; we should serve each other wherever we are, because Jesus came first to serve us.

One of the greatest tragedies of our generation is that so many people now see their faith as individualistic rather than communal. They may have an upward relationship with God, but they are resisting the fact that He calls His children inward *together,* into the church. God wants to teach us our true identity: that we aren't wired to be solo operators. We're designed for relationships in community. In Genesis, the very first thing God declared not good was that Adam was alone, without Eve. We're created for relationship because God is relational.

My friends, it is so much easier to unlock resiliency when we have others in our corner, joining us in the struggle and cheering us on. That is why in virtually every sport, there is the important factor of the home-court advantage and also why you have people cheering runners on during marathons. Because of our relational natures, people help us. And Jesus created the church not only for His glory but also for our edification. People build us up and help us get through.

Catch how the writer of Hebrews ends verse 25: "And so much the more as you see the Day approaching." How encouraging is that? The day of Jesus's return is sooner than it's ever been, right? Jesus's return is nearer than it's ever been in history. Every day it's more important to encourage one another to love and do good.

In other words, as we are together in community, we encourage one another to move outward.

MOVING OUTWARD

Living outward means being on mission on the front lines of God's transformation. Our *upward* relationships with God are the foundation of our hope. The *inward* call of God brings His children together as the church. And the church is designed to move *outward*. In fact, the church is *defined* by that.

It takes resiliency to move outward on mission with Jesus. It's not always easy. There are great things at stake in following Jesus, but walking forward with Him is initiated and sustained by our relationships with Him. The Lord's own steadfastness pushes us forward no matter the cost.

If we want to be fancy,[12] we can call living outward the *Missio Dei*, which means the "mission of God."[13] One of the greatest explanations of that is found in Genesis 12:1–3, when God is speaking to Abraham. We learn that the mission of God is this: for His people to understand that He has blessed us so that we can be a blessing to others. First John 4:11 puts it almost the exact same way: We love others because God first loved us. The Great Commission in Matthew 28 tells us,

> Jesus came and spoke to them, saying, "All authority has been given to Me in heaven and on earth. Go therefore and make disciples of all the nations, baptizing them in the name of the Father and of the Son and of the Holy Spirit, teaching them to observe all things that I have commanded you. (verses 18–20)

Luke 10:1–3 reads,

> After these things the Lord appointed seventy others also, and sent them two by two before His face into every city and place where He Himself was about to go. Then He said to them, "The harvest truly is great, but the laborers are few; therefore pray the Lord of the harvest to send out

---

[12] And we do, naturally!

[13] Isn't it weird that while *mission of God* sounds cool, *Missio Dei* sounds even cooler cause it's Latin?

laborers into His harvest. Go your way; behold, I
send you out as lambs among wolves."

And in Acts 1:8, Jesus says,

> You shall receive power when the Holy Spirit has
> come upon you; and you shall be witnesses to Me
> in Jerusalem, and in all Judea and Samaria, and to
> the end of the earth.

See that? The church is defined, by Jesus Himself, as a
group of people who move outward into the world. Now, if
you've been around church for any length of time, you know
that it has often been pigeonholed as a group of people who
get together to sing and study the Bible. Although those
things are important, a big part of our lives on earth is about
moving outward as well. It's like the third image in our Isaiah verse: "Those who wait on the LORD . . . shall walk and
not faint" (Isaiah 40:31). We're being called, through God's
strength, to "walk the walk" and not just "talk the talk" of
being Christians who attend church.

In times of uncertainty, people who've been blessed—and
who see their blessing as a way to bless other people—stand
out in a good way! There are millions of simple, practical
ways for each of us to go bless others with what God has
given us. Not just in our churches and homes but on our
streets and in our cities.

When people are afraid, they are hungry for the things of
God. Fear comes when we're at the end of our human inge-
nuity. It's when we reach the limit of what we can offer as
humans that we understand we have the gifts of God to offer.

"Hey, listen, I'm praying for you." When was the last time you told someone that?

"Hey, listen, I believe in Jesus. He's changed my life. Have you thought about Him recently?"

"Hey, listen, God loves you, and so do I. I'm here for you. Is there any way I can help you?"

God has blessed us so that we can be a blessing. Even when life is uncertain. Especially when times are tough.

Here's another piece of the outward-moving Missio Dei. Understand what God is telling us in Exodus 19:3–6:

> Moses went up to God, and the LORD called to him from the mountain, saying, "Thus you shall say to the house of Jacob, and tell the children of Israel: 'You have seen what I did to the Egyptians, and how I bore you on eagles' wings and brought you to Myself. Now therefore, if you will indeed obey My voice and keep My covenant, then you shall be a special treasure to Me above all people; for all the earth is Mine. And you shall be to Me a kingdom of priests and a holy nation.' "

We will be a kingdom of priests and a holy nation! Now, the idea of the priests in the Old Testament was that they had a twofold job: They stood before God in the name of the people, and they stood before the people in the name of God. In many ways, the priests functioned as intermediaries, talking to the people about who God is and then talking to God about the needs of the people.

In this cultural moment, in this context for renewal, God wants us to join Jesus, our great High Priest. God wants us to take the needs of our community, the needs of our world, and stand before Him and say, "Father, will You do an amazing work?" The outward movement of the church is service and good works, absolutely: water for the thirsty, company for the imprisoned, care for the bereft, and so on. But just as essentially, the outward movement of the church is intercession. It's prayer and fasting for what is happening in our communities and in the world.

I've heard some people say, "While you're busy praying, I'm out there actually doing things." But that isn't quite right. We pray, and then we work. We pray as we work.[14] We pray after we work, when we are tired and need energy and encouragement and renewal, when we wake up, and before we go to sleep.[15] Like the biblical priests, we stand before God with the needs of our loved ones, with the needs of our community, and with the needs of our world, and then we leave the presence of God and go before the people. We testify to what God has done and will do. We do His work, even as we speak of His goodness and help bring it into action.

And it brings us back full circle. Mounting up with wings like eagles. Running and not being weary. Walking and not fainting. From upward to inward, from inward to outward, and always driven back, upward, into the love of our heavenly Father.

---

[14]   The Benedictine monks had a saying: "Ora et labora." In Latin, that meant, "Pray and work." They viewed the two as inseparable partners, like two sides of one coin.

[15]   This is what Paul means when he says to "pray without ceasing" in 1 Thessalonians 5:17.

YOUR CONTEXT FOR RENEWAL

I'm here to tell you that God wants to do a work of renewal in us. God wants to do something fresh. Renewal brings with it the passing of the old things, right? The Bible teaches that if anyone is in Christ, that person is a new creation. Right here, right now, there are old things that need to pass away in our lives so that what God wants to do can spring up.

This is your context for renewal.

Go upward. Put your hope in God. Wait on God. Call out to God. Those who do that *will* be renewed. He cannot wait for you to spend time with Him. He cannot wait for you to experience His love and joy.

Go inward as the church. You aren't on this journey alone. You're meant to do it with others. Since we want to go far, we've got to go together.

Then go outward. Find ways to bless your community and your world in the name of Jesus. God is in the transformation business, and He wants us to join Him in the Missio Dei, blessing others as we have been blessed.

It takes grit. But I believe that as we continue to grow upward, inward, and outward, we will see renewal not only in ourselves but in our communities, our countries, and our world.

Unlocking Resilience

1. What would it look like for you to invest daily in growing in intimacy with Jesus?

2. Join a local church and become engaged in the ministry there. Don't quit when it gets challenging.

3. Begin to push out into the world in Jesus's name. Pick a place of pain and be Jesus's hands and feet.

6

FIGHTING THE BATTLE AGAINST FEAR AND WORRY

Worry does not empty tomorrow of its sorrow. It empties today of its strength.

—Corrie ten Boom, *Clippings from My Notebook*

We're all scared. Worried. Fearful about the present and the future.

And the frustrating thing is that our humanity limits what we can know. Without the benefit of unlimited wisdom and insight that only God has, we're stuck with an unlimited number of things we can lose sleep over.

What's going to happen at our jobs?

Will things we've done in the past come back to haunt us?

Will we get sick? Get healthy?

What do our friends *really* think about us?

How will our kids turn out?

Does God really love us? Even when we're suffering?

I had to force myself to write only six lines, because the truth is that we could list things that worry us or scare us for what feels like forever.

Don't worry about a thing, 'cause every little thing gonna be all right.

–Bob Marley and the Wailers, "Three Little Birds"

Fear and worry are common to all of us. They're part of the human condition.[1] And the year 2020 not only highlighted our worry and anxiety but also put it into overdrive.

But God doesn't want to leave us there. We can come to the Bible and find our *true north*. Scripture grounds us by giving us an unmoving point to help us orient our messy lives as we journey through this world. It's not by chance that the Bible tells us "Do not fear" more than a few times. Actually, it's 365 times, believe it or not—I think God's trying to tell us something.

It shouldn't surprise us that God knows our struggles. God is God. He created us, and He knows our capacity to deal with fear and worry. Be honest with me for a minute:

---

[1]   Not to mention there are all sorts of clinical versions of fear and worry as well. More than fifteen million American adults suffer from social anxiety disorder. Forty-one percent of employees experience workplace anxiety. More than half of college students asked for help for their anxiety problems. See Mira Rakicevic, "33 Worrisome Anxiety Statistics and Facts for 2021," Disturbmenot!, January 2, 2021, https://disturbmenot.co/anxiety-statistics.

How often do you struggle to trust Him in the day-to-day experiences you have?

But here's the cool part: He already knows we worry, *and* He's okay with it. God promises that He's got the situation under control. We just need to trust him.

Do not worry. . . . Which of you by worrying can add one cubit to his stature?

−Jesus, Matthew 6:25, 27

You could be an Enneagram 13 with an orange wing[2] or an LMNOP on the Myers-Briggs Type Indicator,[3] but either way, you still worry.

It's inside our anxieties that God shows up and reminds us that He's already given us victory over fear and worry. He tells us in 1 John 4:18 that "perfect love casts out fear." And Jesus is that perfect love. The best part is that He has already come. He has already been victorious.

I imagine you're saying you've heard it before. But how do we actually live that out? We have to learn how to trust that victory. And that is where resilience comes from: continuing on, knowing that the victory has been won, sometimes rest-

---

[2] If you know the Enneagram at all, you know I am having fun with you.

[3] Same for you Myers-Briggs folks. I'm an equal opportunity kind of jokester.

ing in it and sometimes allowing it to push us forward. Worry won't add one-tenth of one inch to how tall we are (see Matthew 6:27). Giving our worries to God, though, will teach us that we aren't in control. And that's a good thing.

You see, we have an underlying need to feel in control of our lives. When we feel out of control, we worry, we are anxious, and we become overwhelmed, stuck, and lost. Don't get me wrong—it is helpful to have some control. But what is infinitely better is that God has given us a picture of what life can be like without the worry and anxiety. This life, the abundant life, is available to us only when we lean into trusting Him.

Our ability to persevere does not mean a life devoid of worry; it means a resilient life that allows anxiety, viewed through the lens of the Spirit, to become a type of fuel that keeps us moving forward. We progress through the issues, incorporating many precious lessons learned into what the Lord has for us.

Sorrow looks back, Worry looks around, Faith looks up.

–Ralph Waldo Emerson, *Self-Reliance and Other Essays*

So let's start with this foundation for fighting fear and worry:

We need to abide in faith, hope, and love.
We need a life-giving connection to Jesus.
We need to trust Him.

We'll see this more later in the book, but because we trust Jesus, we have only positive expectations. So in the face of fear and worry, we *will* have an unstoppable hope. Our hope in Jesus plays itself out as we put feet on our hope and live with grit. We aren't just hanging on for dear life (though we certainly feel that way sometimes!), but we're marching toward our goals, keeping the long view in mind, and remembering our experiences with God and His faithfulness.

In this way of living, we will walk out the victory that Jesus bought for us and has applied to our hearts by the Holy Spirit.

7

HOPE HAS A NAME

JOHN 14:1-6

How can we choose hope in times of uncertainty? Because hope isn't an abstract concept. Hope is a person, and hope has a name. As followers of Jesus, we know that He must be the center of our lives. Because He is always faithful, we live with an unstoppable hope.

I remember when we got pregnant with our second child and we found out we were having a girl.[1] We were blown away. First our son, Obadiah, and now a daughter. We couldn't have been happier. It was like it was scripted in a storybook.

I'd always wanted to name our first daughter Maranatha. I could just picture her: this tiny, perfect, brown-and-curly-haired Italian darling. Lynn was on board with the name, but before naming our baby, we had to *meet* her first. With a substantial name like Maranatha, it needed to fit. Part of the excitement of the moment of her birth was seeing exactly

---

[1] I mean, *Lynn* got pregnant. I was a part of it, and it was awesome.

what kind of human we'd cooked up. And the second we laid eyes on her, we agreed: She was a *total* Maranatha.

There's just something about getting a name right, isn't there? And I want to share something very powerful with you about a name.

A name denotes a nature. What I mean is that when the Bible speaks of God's name, it always denotes His character, personality, and nature. We shouldn't get caught up in the spelling or pronunciation of that name. It's really about who the name represents.

When I think of my children—Obadiah, Maranatha, and Annabelle—I think of them as people. I don't think about the letters or the pronunciation of their names. I think about who and how they are.

I have something special to tell you.

When we think about hope, we have a tendency to think of hope as a concept or a construct. Some may even think of hope as a goal to achieve or a destination to pursue.

But I believe something even more amazing.

Hope has a name.

FAITH CURES A TROUBLED HEART

I was in college when my mom was sick with cancer. As the disease progressed, there were many nights when she would struggle to sleep, and most nights when I was home, I'd try to stay up with her.[2] She'd ask me to read the Bible to her, and John 14 was one of her favorite sections. I didn't know the Lord at that time, but I read it so much that eventually I memorized most of that chapter. I didn't know it then, but

---

[2]   As a college student, I pretty much majored in staying up all night.

those words from Jesus would stick deep inside me, and I'd return to them time and time again whenever uncertainty or pain would weigh me down.

So listen to what Jesus was saying to my mom (and me) and what He's saying now to you:

> "Let not your heart be troubled; you believe in God, believe also in Me. In My Father's house are many mansions; if it were not so, I would have told you. I go to prepare a place for you. And if I go and prepare a place for you, I will come again and receive you to Myself; that where I am, there you may be also. And where I go you know, and the way you know."
>
> Thomas said to Him, "Lord, we do not know where You are going, and how can we know the way?"
>
> Jesus said to him, "I am the way, the truth, and the life. No one comes to the Father except through Me." (verses 1–6)

Faith is what cures a troubled heart. That's so beautiful that I want to say it again: Faith cures a troubled heart.

Is your heart troubled right now? We have so many reasons to be troubled. Each of us has our own fears and doubts. As I like to say, *all God's children got issues.* So it's no surprise when we look at what's going on in the world and we're like, "Ugh, how is this all going to work out? Or *is* it?"

To which Jesus says, "Let not your heart be troubled." Why? What gives Jesus the authority to say that?

Check out what He says next: "You believe in God, believe

also in Me." This is why I say that faith cures a troubled heart. Jesus is not asking us to carry the confusion and the disappointment. He is telling us that He came to earth for a reason—that He lived a perfect life and died on the cross and was raised from the dead for a reason.

God absolutely *loves* it when we trust in Jesus. Here's what the writer of Hebrews says in chapter 11, verses 1 and 6:

> Faith is the substance of things hoped for, the evidence of things not seen. . . .

> But without faith it is impossible to please [God], for he who comes to God must believe that He is, and that He is a rewarder of those who diligently seek Him.

Our generation is so used to walking by sight, not by faith.[3]

The problem is that walking by sight undercuts our ability to unlock resilience. Why is that a problem? Because we have to be resilient to experience something that we cannot see. Resilience is born by a vision of what can be but is not yet.

God wants us to walk by faith, by trusting in Jesus. That is why we're exploring the unstoppable life, a life fueled by hope and grit, because even right now I believe Jesus is saying to all of us, to our whole country and the whole world, something like, "Listen, your hearts *are* troubled. But don't be troubled. You believe in God, so believe in Me."

---

[3]   Here's the funny thing: A lot of the stuff we believe because we "see" it is actually false, but that's a topic for another day.

The only true way to believe in God the Father is to believe in God the Son. And God the Son—Jesus—says that by knowing Him, we will know His Father. That's why it's so important for us to exercise the faith God has already given us. And like a muscle, our faith will get stronger the more we exercise it.

Lord, You know my heart is troubled right now, but I believe in You. I know You've got this. That's how we exercise our faith.

Jesus, help me. I don't have anyone else to turn to. That's how we grow our faith.

YOU ARE INVITED

The book of Hebrews tells us that we can't please God unless we have faith.

That sounds scary, maybe even unfair. Like, what if we're in a place where we don't have a lot of faith? Does that mean that the super-holy people with tons of faith will please God the most and the rest of us will be able to please Him only a tiny bit or even not at all?

But that isn't how it works. Faith is a gift God gives us (see Ephesians 2:8–9). We don't have to manufacture it ourselves. We don't get faith if we are smart enough or work hard enough or attend church seven Sundays in a row. God has given us the gift of faith, and we can choose to use that gift in ways that please Him. It doesn't matter whether our faith is the size of a tiny little mustard seed or a huge vat of mustard from Costco—either way, we can still exercise our faith to please God.

I appreciate how the apostle Paul puts it: "God has chosen the foolish things of the world to put to shame the wise, and

God has chosen the weak things of the world to put to shame the things which are mighty" (1 Corinthians 1:27). Feeling weak or foolish? Full of doubts and worries? God can work with that. He *will* work with that! What He is asking us to do is take the step—to walk in faith, every day, and watch what He does in our lives.

And walking by faith is the essence of the grit we've been talking about.

Grit shows itself through our simple, faithful steps. We keep walking forward with Jesus, we keep moving in the direction He has shown us, because we trust that everything will work out if we just keep going.[4]

One way I can always tell that I'm not exercising my faith enough is when my insides are turbulent and uncertain. That's when any little bit of negativity—some bad news, a stressful situation, whatever—will start me fretting and worrying and overanalyzing. Freaking out inside, basically.

My bride, Lynn, is the best when I'm like that. "Daniel," she'll remind me, "God's not negative."

She's so right. Jesus died for us so we can have a life better than we ever dreamed (see John 10:10). God doesn't love us and grow us by pumping fear and worry into our hearts; He loves us by inviting us to use the faith in our hearts. And, remember, that faith is God's gift to us. For me, it's like I sense Him saying, "Daniel, you're freaking out here, but *I'm* not freaked out. I've seen this already. I know what I'm going to do in this situation. So, Daniel, you don't have to be troubled here, but you *do* need to remember to trust Me."

I believe that every moment of our lives is an invitation

---

[4] Or as Dory from *Finding Nemo* would say, "Just keep swimming."

from God to trust Him. Seriously, every moment! How cool is that? It's always the right time to see that God is not just a good Father but a good, *good* Father.[5] God isn't just sort of good; He's amazingly good! And those moments when our hearts are troubled are the times when we learn to walk by faith and not by sight—when we experience that faith cures a troubled heart.

So the key for each of us is to accept Jesus's invitation in our times of struggle and fear. We must learn to identify the negativity as an opportunity to draw closer to Him. And we must keep on taking those steps of faith, even as we continue to grapple with our own doubts.

This can become the "secret sauce" of life in the Spirit— when we see every situation as God's invitation. This is how we experience God at street level. We accept that invitation by simply saying yes to Jesus in the midst of whatever is happening. We find ourselves saying, "Yes, Lord. I am Your servant. Lead and guide me."

The issue for many is that we fail to identify the opportunities. I know this all too well. We get caught up in our heads and take the downward spiral away from Jesus into the negativity. We focus on the problems and obsess over our fears about them. But as we are led by the Spirit, we resist the impulse to focus on the problems and instead focus on Jesus.

Then, finally, we live resiliently in hope as we respond to Jesus in concrete, tangible ways. We take the steps that He invites us to take. We take these steps in the face of our fears. These faith steps become the fulfillment of God's will for us,

---

[5] Shout-out to Pat Barrett and co-writer Anthony Brown for a great song!

and ultimately we get to experience the unfolding of His plan!

IN LIGHT OF ETERNITY

Another thing John 14 teaches us is this: If we don't see our stresses and struggles in the context of eternity, we aren't *really* seeing them.

I mess this up all the time. I'll look at something that's bugging me, like just about every time someone does something differently than I would have done it. Or I'll focus on something that's hurting me or hurting people I love, like any of the countless injustices that we see every day, and I'll think, *I hate this and it needs to stop.*

And in a sense, it *does* need to stop. Pain for pain's sake is meaningless. And suffering will stop—if not now, then in eternity. It isn't wrong to try to end suffering or stress.

But when we pay attention to *only* our present context, we're not seeing the full picture God wants to show us. He's got much more in store.

There are so many examples of this. A child is disciplined so he will grow into a well-adjusted young man.[6] A skier punishes her body and mind in the summer and fall so she can win trophies in the winter. A child of God gives generously to their local church so they can develop a heart that trusts God and directs His resources to change the world.

When it comes to us, though, we forget those lessons all the time. It's as if we believe that long-term context—and

---

[6] Just to be clear, in case you wondered, I'm not talking about any sort of abuse. I'm talking about simple, loving correction by a grace-filled parent.

even eternal context—matter, except in our specific cases. Then it's all about erasing our pain and solving suffering now. But the Bible always invites us to take the long view. Taking the long view is what *God* does, and it's what we're called to do as well. One way I think we can preach good news to ourselves in this area is by looking back on our lives. For most of us, there is at least one moment of deep pain in our stories, and for most of us, life is better than it was at that moment. For some of us, life is a lot better. So remembering our worst moment often shows us how temporary it was.

Jesus can redeem even our most painful circumstances, things we have gone through that we will maybe never understand. For some of you, this sounds like I'm crazy. I confess I don't know how God does it, but I know that He can. I've seen it.

I also know that in heaven, every tear will be wiped away from every eye (see Revelation 21:4). So even if you cannot fathom how God will take your tragedy and bring beauty out of it, now more than ever I want to encourage you to hope against hope and to keep taking that next step and moving forward, whatever it takes.

You absolutely know that you are gonna make it when you keep taking the next step. Life is a miraculous journey. And it doesn't just *happen* to us. We need to keep on going, moving forward, no matter what.

ETERNITY IS THE REALEST THING

I find that for so many people, eternity can be hard to remember or even to see as real.[7] But eternity isn't just a concept or

---

7   To be honest, I find that I have to work to remember eternity.

idea. Seeing our present struggles in the light of eternity means realizing that eternity is the realest thing that exists. It is real, right now, and will always be. Throughout the Bible, God talks about our lives being eternal. Everybody will live eternally, and Jesus will bring His own to His Father's mansion. That's why we can't afford to let our present fears shipwreck us. Getting eternity right is the most important thing. Listen to how Paul agonizes over this in Philippians 1:21–24:

> To me, to live is Christ, and to die is gain. But if I live on in the flesh, this will mean fruit from my labor; yet what I shall choose I cannot tell. For I am hard-pressed between the two, having a desire to depart and be with Christ, which is far better. Nevertheless to remain in the flesh is more needful for you.

Paul knows that faith is a matter of life and death. He's torn. On the one hand, he longs to be with Jesus in his forever home. On the other hand, though, he's walking with Jesus by faith as he lives, and he's doing good work with and for his friends and his enemies. Either way—whether he lives or dies—he knows that he'll experience God's eternal, unending love.

The crazy part is that Paul is writing this *while he's in jail.* And not just overnight. For *years.* So he's not even sure where his next meal is coming from, let alone whether he's going to make it out alive and be able to continue ministering.

Does that sound familiar? Maybe not the exact details, but the uncertainty? The hopelessness hanging over your head?

There's never a wrong time to remind ourselves of the good news of God. Jesus has gone ahead to prepare a place for us. Through the work of Christ on the cross, God has forgiven our sins and has prepared us for eternity by sharing the righteousness of Jesus with us.

But here's the truth: The good news of God isn't that we have to get everything right. The good news is that Jesus got everything right. And right now, Jesus is sharing that righteousness with us in a way that transforms us on earth and prepares us for heaven.

Like Paul, let's live in such a way that we can say, "As long as I live, I'm living in light of God's presence and love, and when I die, I know I'm going home."

Talk about hope and grit! Our lives matter in the here and now. But in a way, they matter only because of their relation to eternity. Today, next week, next month—what we do is connected to an unending future.

Anyone who knows me will tell you I'm not big on math. I can count music notes, but that's about it.[8] However, even *I* can compare finite time to eternity and realize the difference. Our life on earth compared to the unending afterlife. Ten years or a hundred years on earth compared to being with Jesus in heaven forever. It's like a drop of water compared to the ocean.

HOPE IS HERE, AND HOPE IS COMING BACK

Now, you've maybe seen the funny bumper sticker "Jesus is coming soon . . . look busy!"

---

[8]   I want to formally apologize to my kids. High school math is way beyond my abilities. Again, you guys, I am sorry!

I have to laugh at that because it reminds me of my family, like if Lynn and one of our kids are out doing errands and I'm at home with our other kids and we start a little food fight in the kitchen while making Rice Krispie Treats. When we hear the sound of the garage door opening, it's panic time. "Mom's home! We gotta get busy and clean this up!"

But really that bumper sticker isn't good theology. It's not how we should be thinking about God. God *already* sees everything we do, so it's not about trying to trick Him. Here's how the apostle Paul puts it in Romans 13:11–12:

> Do this, knowing the time, that now it is high time to awake out of sleep; for now our salvation is nearer than when we first believed. The night is far spent, the day is at hand. Therefore let us cast off the works of darkness, and let us put on the armor of light.

So we need to ask ourselves, Are we awake, or are we sleepwalking through life?

Because Jesus *is* coming back. That doesn't mean we should look busy, but it does mean we want to live right. Maybe we've been involved in activities we're not supposed to be involved in. Maybe there are things that we need to stop doing but we just haven't stopped. And Jesus is inviting us to walk as children of light, in the light, instead of doing shady things under the cover of darkness.[9]

---

[9] Remember, this isn't about doing good things so God will save you. It's about being accepted by God, in Christ, and allowing that to change your actions.

I realize you probably are like, "Fusco, you seem like a decent guy. Maybe even a semi-intelligent guy.[10] But do you *really* believe, honestly, that Jesus is coming back to earth?" That's a totally fair question, and I've heard it often. Even from people who believe in Jesus and believe in the Bible. All of us have red lines in our heads or hearts that feel uncrossable, right? For some it's the concept of the Virgin Birth. For others it's not understanding how a supposedly all-powerful God could allow so much evil to happen. Some people's red line is the literal return of Jesus. And I'm not here to prove with some airtight logic or irrefutable scientific proof what exactly will happen. There's always going to be some faith involved in choosing to follow Jesus and taking Him at His word. But I do want to hold up the idea to the light and maybe look at it from another angle. How can a guy who lived two thousand years ago[11] come back?

Great question! But check this out: If the existence of God is possible, then anything supernatural is on the menu. Especially something like the second coming of Jesus. I get it if someone wants to go full atheist/materialist. If nothing can exist beyond the interactions of atoms, then yeah, Jesus can't really come back to earth. But the minute you are open to something beyond the physical, you're open to the return of Jesus.

---

[10] Thanks for the hypothetical compliment! You could also add, "You should star in the next Christopher Nolan action movie!" and "You are quite handsome."

[11] At least that's *one* thing no one disagrees about. There most definitely was a dude named Jesus who walked around ancient Palestine teaching people.

The first coming of Jesus to earth changed everything. Then His death changed everything. And then His resurrection changed it all again.

The early church existed and grew *because* they knew in their bones that Jesus had been killed (they'd seen that part) and then had come back to life (many of them had also seen *that* part). Jesus appeared to many of His disciples between His resurrection and ascension into heaven. They'd seen the body . . . but then they saw the empty tomb, and the tomb's previous resident started showing up to their meetings and having dinner with them! The disciples also saw Jesus physically ascend into heaven (see Luke 24:51)![12] And following that, He even appeared to more than five hundred people at one time.

And just like He rose again and appeared to hundreds, He is coming back. Look, I'm a Christian pastor, and I believe God is real and active. So for me, and for any believer, the return of Jesus is absolutely possible at any moment. I know He's alive, and I know He promised to return. And I'm so glad, because when I look around at everything that's happening in the world, I can see that the only true hope for all of us is the return of Jesus.

Jesus is coming back, and He's going to make everything right. He's going to unbreak every broken thing—every heart, every relationship, every part of creation that is groaning and crying out. This is what the Bible promises about what's coming: "God will wipe away every tear from their eyes; there shall be no more death, nor sorrow, nor crying.

---

[12] Every time I think of this, I just wish the apostles had a cell phone camera. What a video that would have been!

There shall be no more pain, for the former things have passed away" (Revelation 21:4).

And Jesus wants those who believe in Him to be absolutely *pumped* that He's preparing a place for us before He comes back to welcome us home: "In My Father's house are many mansions; if it were not so, I would have told you. I go to prepare a place for you. And if I go and prepare a place for you, I will come again and receive you to Myself; that where I am, there you may be also" (John 14:2–3).

That coming reality serves as an ever-present hope for us and something that fuels our desire to keep going, especially as we believe in and follow the one true Hope.

THIS IS THE WAY

Because we know that Jesus is coming back, today is the day—whether for the first time or the thousandth—to walk in the right direction. To walk with Jesus toward eternity.

Life gets real if we let these kinds of questions in: What does it look like for you today to walk with Jesus toward eternity? How is God inviting you to take that next step?

You can't miss how important resilience is on this journey either. When you remember that you are being invited into eternity, you just keep taking the next steps. You realize that some steps are easy and some are hard. Some steps are joyful and others are filled with fear. But you keep on taking the steps. This is what having perseverance, grit, and resilience is all about.

I love what happens in verse 5 of our passage. Jesus has just said, "You know the way I'm going." And then Thomas pops up and is like, "Actually, we *don't* know the way You're going, so how are we supposed to follow You?"

Thomas gets a bad rap sometimes, but isn't he just asking questions the others are afraid to ask? And here's how Jesus answers his honest question: "*I* am the way." See, Thomas knew Jesus, and Jesus told him that was the only thing he needed to know.

It's the only thing *we* need to know.

My friends, hope has a name, and His name is Jesus—the same Jesus who is the way, the truth, and the life. So we follow Jesus. We trust in Him. We believe He is the truth. And Jesus isn't just *my* truth or *your* truth, as we often hear people say in our culture. There's actually no such thing as *my* truth or *your* truth—those are just our opinions! Jesus isn't an opinion. He is *the* truth. And because Jesus is the way and Jesus is the truth, Jesus is the life.

Here's what the apostle Paul says in Colossians 1:27: "To them God willed to make known what are the riches of the glory of this mystery among the Gentiles: which is Christ in you, the hope of glory." Our hope of a glorious eternity rests on the fact of who Jesus is. And that's the secret to a persevering, resilient life. In uncertain times, in times of trouble, in unprecedented and fear-filled times, we need to remember that Jesus is the way, the truth, and the life and that no one can come to the Father except through Jesus.

Now, I realize those are fighting words in our culture. We live in a day and age where we're told that every path leads to heaven, if heaven even exists in the first place. But if Jesus had said that every road led to the top of the mountain, He never would have been whipped and beaten and nailed to a cross. In the Garden of Gethsemane before His crucifixion, He never would have sweat drops of blood and asked His

Father if there were any other way besides the Cross that people could come to God.

And I can only imagine as a father myself that when Jesus said, "My Father, if it is possible, let this cup pass from Me" (Matthew 26:39), if there were really another way, God would have said (with that booming voice we all imagine He uses), "No worries, my Son. This is only one of hundreds of ways to get to heaven. You can drop that crossbeam and come up to heaven now. I think Your sinless life has been enough of an example for people to see what we are all about. It sounds like this Via Dolorosa thing is getting to be too much."

But that didn't happen. If there were any other way for us to be brought back to God, eternally, Jesus never would have had to die for us. Not all roads lead to heaven. Only Jesus—the way, the truth, and the life—leads us into God's eternal family.

When our hearts are troubled by our present struggles, let's remember that life is an eternal journey, and let's always look at life through the lens of eternity. Jesus has never been closer to coming back than today. Let's keep our eyes open and walk closely with Jesus, who is the way, the truth, and the life. He hasn't written off a single one of us, and He never will.

He is extending His hand to each of us, because no one else can bring us to the Father. No one else can take us where we truly long to go. It may be a long journey or a short one, but it will begin and end in Hope.

Unlocking Resilience

1. When you are feeling anxious or nervous, how can you invite Jesus into the middle of your situation?

2. How does the reality of eternity energize your ability to walk by faith through the struggles of your life?

3. If Jesus is the way, where should you be following Him right now?

THE CURE FOR FEAR

ISAIAH 41:8-10

Even in the best of times, there are so many things we fear. In uncertain times, our fear can feel overwhelming. But the beautiful thing is that followers of Jesus don't need to let fear take control. God offers us a cure for fear.

I've said it before, but you'd better get used to it: *Hope has a name.* When our hope is Jesus and that hope is bound to our grit, it can be unstoppable. But what about fear? Sometimes the fear we feel is so real, so heavy, so *everywhere,* that we can't help but sink into it despite our hope.

There's an awesome story in Matthew 14 about that. Jesus's closest followers (we know them as the disciples) have been up all night in a boat, riding out a storm. And as they are battling the wind and waves, in the eerie light before dawn, they see Jesus walking toward them on the water. Naturally, they freak out, thinking they're seeing a ghost. But Jesus lets them know it's Him and tells them to be brave.

Peter is like, "Prove it, Lord. If it's really You, tell me to walk across the water to You."[1] Talk about courageous faith!

And Jesus simply says, "Come."

And Peter climbs out of the boat, sets his feet on the water,[2] and walks toward Jesus (see verses 28–29). That's when it gets interesting. Here's how Matthew finishes the story:

> When he saw that the wind was boisterous, he was afraid; and beginning to sink he cried out, "Lord, save me!"
>
> And immediately Jesus stretched out His hand and caught him, and said to him, "O you of little faith, why did you doubt?" And when they got into the boat, the wind ceased.
>
> Then those who were in the boat came and worshiped Him, saying, "Truly You are the Son of God." (verses 30–33)

Fear happens because we're human. It's what we *do* with our fear that matters.

Peter began to sink when his fear overtook his courage and hope. But how many of us would have been too scared to step out of the boat at all?[3] Fear is simply how we humans

---

[1]   Gosh, I just love Peter. So boisterous and bossy. When God got ahold of his heart, amazing things happened. Before that, he was kind of a train wreck, like the rest of us.

[2]   What in the *world* would that have been like?

[3]   Let alone ask Jesus for permission to walk on the water like He did!

react to uncertainty and danger. Maybe you're a parent who can barely watch their kid ride a bike down a hill. Maybe you just wake up in the middle of the night freaked out about the future. We all experience fear, even if we're resiliently following Jesus and living in hope.

So the real question is, When we experience fear, what follows? What does Jesus want to do in our lives when we are afraid?

That's where the rubber meets the road. Jesus is working and we are responding. That is an important idea when you follow Jesus. There is what we do, and there is what Jesus wants to do. And, ultimately, we bring our fears to Jesus and get to enjoy watching how He is going to work.

CHOSEN AND CALLED

Let's dive into these amazing verses from Isaiah 41 to see what they can teach us about fear and how God wants to operate in our lives:

> You, Israel, are My servant,
> Jacob whom I have chosen,
> The descendants of Abraham My friend.
> You whom I have taken from the ends of the earth,
> And called from its farthest regions,
> And said to you,
> "You are My servant,
> I have chosen you and have not cast you away:
> Fear not, for I am with you;
> Be not dismayed, for I am your God.
> I will strengthen you,

Yes, I will help you,
I will uphold you with My righteous right hand."
    (verses 8–10)

This message came to God's people at a precarious time. Rival governments were putting pressure on their land. There were military conflicts. A succession of kings—some good, some bad—were unable to make a real difference. The people were watching their culture crumble.

It was at that point that God raised up the prophet Isaiah to let the people know the solution to their trials. You're going to love this: God had chosen a simple solution, which was that they needed to step up and serve others, just as God has chosen those of us who believe in Jesus—the worldwide church—to serve. We're scared, we're being pressured and attacked from what seems like every side, and the way out is to lean into serving others. And that's amazingly good news!

Wait. Hang on. *Serving?* It's good news that we're called to be servants?

I haven't met too many people who are like, "You know, the only thing I want to do right now is serve people." If we're being honest, most of us want to *be* served.

I know it sounds counterintuitive, but when we follow Jesus and simply respond to Him, we realize that the more confident we are that our identity is in Christ, the more we identify with His humility and willingness to serve.

I'll never forget watching my friend Luis Palau live out this reality. Luis had been struggling for some time with cancer when he also began having heart problems. Even while he was in the hospital, he was sharing the good news of Jesus, as was always Luis's way. He was continually looking out for the spiritual well-being of those who were tasked with his physical well-being.

As Luis struggled with his health, he sent me text messages to encourage me in the ministry—scriptures that the Lord had laid on his heart for me and a gentle reminder to focus on the most important things (Jesus, my wife, and my children) in the midst of busy ministry seasons. Luis was serving me, even as his body was breaking down.

When Luis was finally released from the hospital, with only a few weeks left on earth, he wanted to spend individual time with each of his grandchildren. He had a word for each of them, and, like Jacob blessing his sons, he wanted to bless his grandchildren. And all this took place during his last few weeks this side of eternity.[4]

My friend Luis's story reminds me of when two of Jesus's disciples, James and John, were angling for places of honor and authority. They figured Jesus was setting up an earthly government, and they wanted to be the ones sitting on the left and the right of His throne. Of course, word got back to the other disciples, and they were *not* happy with James and John.[5] But Jesus wasn't interested in solving their little intra-disciple squabble. Instead, He used it as an opportunity to call them together and go deep into the meaning of life and eternity.

---

4   Luis Palau went home to be with Jesus on March 11, 2021. I sure miss him.

5   I always have assumed that the other disciples were actually upset that they didn't think to ask Jesus for those positions first!

When the ten heard it, they began to be greatly displeased with James and John. But Jesus called them to Himself and said to them, "You know that those who are considered rulers over the Gentiles lord it over them, and their great ones exercise authority over them. Yet it shall not be so among you; but whoever desires to become great among you shall be your servant. And whoever of you desires to be first shall be slave of all. For even the Son of Man did not come to be served, but to serve, and to give His life as ransom for many." (Mark 10:41–45)

Now, I know that's the right way to think, but, cards on the table, it can be a real struggle to avoid wanting authority and importance. Not that I usually ask for anything as grand as James and John did! Few of us would go that far. We know it's not right to pray, "Father, can I be more important than everyone else?"

But what James and John were really asking for was power that should be God's—and don't we ask for the same thing? I know *I* do. Every time I think about how someone just won a million dollars in the lottery, I wonder if maybe I should ask God to allow me to win the lottery.[6] It comes from a good place. Wanting to provide for my family is a good thing. But wanting more money than I could ever need is not what it looks like for me to trust God on the daily journey of life.

Or when I pray that God would vindicate me in a situa-

---

[6]   Don't tell me you haven't thought of it before!

tion where I feel that I have been unjustly called out or labeled. Wanting people to know the truth about me is not a problem. But often what I really want is for people to realize that I am not as bad as they think so I can be in a place of honor.

That gets at why I'm so grateful for who Jesus is. Jesus Himself didn't come to earth to be served by us. Rather, He came to serve and to give His life as a ransom—to die on the cross for the sins of the world. Jesus is our example, our model, of the ultimate servant. Only Jesus could die for the sins of the world, it's true, but all those who follow Him can set down their desire for authority and honor and respond in simple service to others.

Why would we do that? Because that service is God's design for *us*—since it renews us and teaches us and disciples us—and for the *world*, since in acts of service we become the hands and heart of God (see Matthew 25:31–46).

Even in times of great fear, our job is still to serve. How can we get out of the boat and take that step on the water? How can we reach out? How can we give? How can we simply become God's love for people who might not otherwise experience it?

My friends, this is how we unlock resilience when life is a mess. We keep on serving. We keep on reaching out. It's simple, just like unlocking a door with a key. But it is something that we must choose to do. When that happens, things open up and the way forward is illuminated.

FEAR CANNOT STAND IN THE PRESENCE OF GOD

It's been a few pages, so I want us to look at Isaiah 41:10 again. We've seen that even when we feel fear and uncertainty, we are God's chosen servants. And serving isn't just a command—it's how we live closest to the example Jesus set for us. This verse brings us to the cure for our fear:

> Fear not, for I am with you;
> Be not dismayed, for I am your God.
> I will strengthen you,
> Yes, I will help you,
> I will uphold you with My righteous right hand.

This is provocative in all the right ways! The open secret that nobody wants to tell you is that we *will* continue to experience fear. That's part of our human nature and part of this fallen world. But what we need to remember is that whenever we feel afraid, at the same time, we are also in the presence of the living God. The Alpha and Omega. All-powerful and all-knowing. Perfect Love. The Prince of Peace. The Great Physician. The Lord Who Heals. The First and the Last. The Great I AM. El Shaddai (the All-Sufficient One). Emmanuel (God with Us). The King of kings and the Lord of lords.

Since *that* God is the God who is with us in our fear, He is saying that the cure for fear is Himself!

We know and serve a miraculous God. Our hearts can rejoice because what seems impossible for us, God can do. He is strong and sovereign. He is absolutely, always certain. And He's got our backs.

So each and every time we feel fear, let's introduce that fear to our God, the ruler of the universe. Let's say, "Lord, You know that I'm fearful, but I know that You're with me. Lord, You know that I believe, but help my unbelief. Lord,

You know that I might be weak in this moment, but in my weakness, Your strength is made perfect."

God has promised that He will never leave us, never walk away. Jesus tells us that He'll always be with us, even to the end of the age. Those are some long-lasting guarantees.[7]

What usually trips us up, though, is focusing on the short term. We may believe God will never forsake us from here to eternity, but we can still forget He is with us in every single moment in between. Even the fear-filled ones. The painful ones. That's why we need to bring our whole heart to God—not just to say the "right" kind of prayer but to pray from the depths of who we really are and what we are really feeling. To lean into the things we are struggling with and really, truly talk to God about it. He *is* present with us, always. Honest prayer can resurface that truth in our hearts. And as we experience God's presence in those moments, fear dissipates.

Listen to how the apostle John puts it in 1 John 4:18–19: "There is no fear in love; but perfect love casts out fear, because fear involves torment. But he who fears has not been made perfect in love. We love Him because He first loved us."

God's perfect love—experienced through the finished work of Jesus, because of the Holy Spirit—casts the fear out of our lives.[8] So when we catch ourselves feeling afraid, that's an opportunity to exercise our faith and walk forward in God's perfect love. We don't pray, "Lord, I want to stop being

---

[7] Eternity is a long time!

[8] I'm not talking about the fear of the Lord. We know that the fear of the Lord is the beginning of wisdom, and that's a healthy part of our relationships with God.

fearful." Instead, we pray, "Lord, when I'm fearful, help me remember You're with me. Will You allow Your perfect love to cast out the fear I feel?"

When I think about great love casting out fear, it reminds me of when I'm watching a movie with our kids and a scary part comes on. Our youngest, Annabelle, usually snuggles in real close to me. Sometimes she even hides her face against me. And I'll just put my arm around her and say, "Sweetie, Daddy's here." And I'll feel her relax—not quite all the way, because that part of the movie is still scary—because in that moment, she knows my presence guarantees she'll be safe.

And you know what? I absolutely love it when she does that! I'm not saying that I pick scary (yet kid-appropriate) movies just so she'll lean in closer to me, but I'm not *not* saying that either.

God is the same way. Lean into Him and let your fears go.

Like children, we can derive strength and resolve just knowing that we are in our Father's arms. God's strength comforts us and propels us forward. Our resilience is not found in our own strength or toughness. It is found in our safety in God's presence.

GOD WITH US

God's presence is our reality.

Here's how Joshua 1:9 puts it: "Have I not commanded you? Be strong and of good courage; do not be afraid, nor be dismayed, for the LORD your God is with you wherever you go."

I love that! Don't fear. Don't be dismayed. Be strong and courageous. Why? Because God is with you wherever you go. God *is* with us. He always has been and always will be. We live in the reality of Emmanuel (God with Us). Day in and day out, minute by minute, God is with us. As we drink coffee and sit in traffic and joke with our kids or find ourselves bewildered following the most recent events of our lives or our world, He is always present. That's what is so great about who Jesus is. Like Eugene Peterson put it in *The Message,* Jesus "moved into the neighborhood" (John 1:14; Revelation 21:3). And the whole reason God did that—does that—is because He loves us. He wants to be near to us. He *is* near to us.

So you and I don't need to let fear sink us. We can let the presence of God lift us.

Here's a simple way to experience the presence of God in a particular circumstance. Try praying something like this: "Lord, let me be aware of Your presence. Open up my heart to the reality that You are always with me, that You are God with me, and that You are the God who loves me."

It's that simple. But don't pray it unless you are ready for your heart to be opened!

PROMISES THAT STRENGTHEN
Here's the final gift these verses have for us. In the second half of Isaiah 41:10, God says to us,

> I will strengthen you,
> Yes, I will help you,
> I will uphold you with My righteous right hand.

My friends, in times of fear, these are the promises we need to trust. And they are extraordinary, aren't they? God's promise is to strengthen us. His affirmation is that He will always help us. His commitment is that He will uphold us—that when we are weak, He is strong.

I love that word *uphold*. It means to confirm, support, or maintain. God promises to support us when we are weak.

I remember a time when I went through a deep valley in my faith. I felt so lost and I was scared. I started to feel as though I was missing the joy that had previously been such an ever-present part of my journey with Jesus. But as I leaned into Him and trusted His plan and His strength, only then did I start to realize that the Father was there, supporting me the whole time. And looking back on that season, I realize He was helping me and holding me up, even when I couldn't hold myself up.

That's what Scripture is promising when it says God will hold us up with His righteous right hand. It's not just any hand—it's His strong right hand. That's what the Bible means when it says He holds us in His right hand. It's His dominant hand, His hand of strength.

Are we trusting in that right now? Or in the promise "that all things work together for good to those who love God, to those who are the called according to His purpose" (Romans 8:28)?[9]

These promises and countless others are given to us by God, and all He is asking of us is that we choose to trust Him.

Now, when it comes to promises, there's a difference between belief and trust. Imagine if a friend of mine makes a chair out of popsicle sticks and asks me to sit on it. I could

---

[9] Check out the rest of Romans 8 to see how this incredible promise unfolds.

take a nice long look at the chair and tell my friend, "Yep! I'm sure that chair you made can hold me up!" But until I sit my lightweight[10] rear down in that chair, I'm not really *trusting* in the chair, right? Maybe my friend is a genius engineer. Maybe my friend is delusional. In either case, my trust is going to lead me to really, truly find out.

That's what God is asking you and me to do with the promises He's given us. (And no, they aren't like popsicle-stick chairs!) God is inviting us to simply respond to Jesus at every turn. It is when we do that we discover the truth of God's promises, because we see them being fulfilled in our own lives and the lives of others.

Remember, God is with us every step of the way! It's like when He's talking to the people of Israel and tells them to be strong and be of good courage. He says that no matter what happens, no matter what they're worried about, He's never going to leave or forsake them (see Deuteronomy 31:6).

God is telling us to be strong and courageous, but are we tuning in to His voice?

I used to say to my kids when they were little, "One, two, three . . . eyes on me," whenever I needed them to focus and hear what I had to say. And God is always saying that to you and me. I believe He wants us to focus on Him and listen to Him. He's with us, right now—me as I write this, you as you read this. He knows all our fears, just like He's numbered every hair on every head (see Luke 12:7).[11] He knows everything about us, and He loves us perfectly.

---

[10] Ahem.

[11] This always totally blows my mind. If you have ever seen a picture or video of me, you realize there are a lot of hairs on this head!

If that sounds scary and you don't know Jesus or you have strayed from closeness to Him, I want to tell you something: God is for you. Always *for* you!

We're sometimes told that God is out to get us. But listen, He is not against you. He already sent Jesus to die on the cross, for you. And here's His motivation for doing so:

> For God so loved the world that He gave His only begotten Son, that whoever believes in Him should not perish but have everlasting life. For God did not send His Son into the world to condemn the world, but that the world through Him might be saved. (John 3:16–17).

That might sound familiar to many of us. But catch how the first six words—*For God so loved the world*—set up everything else. And don't miss what happens in the second sentence either. God didn't send Jesus to get us in trouble. We were already in trouble—more trouble than any of us ever realized. God sent His Son to save the world. That's crazy good news! And it means that whoever you are, wherever you are, whatever you've done, God is absolutely on your side.

There's a saying that God can't love you more and won't love you less. His love for you is already set to maximum, and nothing will change that. And from out of that perfect love, He is asking if you will trust His promises.

One reason we have trouble trusting God's promises is that many people are unreliable. Unfaithful. People say they're going to do all sorts of things they never do. Making a promise is one thing, but keeping it is another. When it comes to promises, actions are what count, not words.

The Lord doesn't make promises that He won't keep. God is not only a promise maker but also a covenant keeper.

I can understand how in today's world you might be skeptical about the idea of God being a covenant keeper. We see so many broken promises as well as people in power or authority breaking the rules left and right. But whenever we start to doubt that God keeps His promises, we need to ask ourselves what happened to make us doubt Him. Throughout Scripture, there are so many places where God looks as though He is doing or allowing things that could undermine His promises. But as time passes and people see a fuller picture, they realize that He has been absolutely true to His promises all along.

Those stories happen today as well. I bet if you think about it, you can remember a time when God fulfilled His promises in your life in a different way than you ever could have imagined.

This reality provokes us to continue forward. The hope that God will work keeps us taking steps forward. And not just tentative steps but bold ones, not necessarily knowing the outcome but knowing He who has a preferred outcome is working out glorious plans. So we keep going, knowing that because of Him, we are gonna make it.

So the question for us right now—in uncertain times, with all our fears, with all our concerns—is, Will we trust Him?

Trust means continuing to walk forward with hope in our hearts. Trust is stepping out into the unknown, knowing the God who has made Himself known. Trust is resiliently moving in the direction pointed out by the Spirit, even in the face of seemingly insurmountable odds.

God wants us to trust Him because He's trustworthy, so

let's step forward in faith and trust Him! Let's respond to Him and see where He leads. If the Bible and our walk with God demonstrate anything to us, it's that His promises aren't limited-time offers that apply in only the good times.

God's promises are a solid rock on which we can build our lives.

God's promises are a harbor that shelters us from even the craziest storm.

God's promises are a banner that reminds us who He is and who we are.

The Lord is inviting us to allow His presence to cure our fear. He wants us to be filled with a joy unspeakable. And the joy of God's presence fuels us to keep on keeping on, no matter the obstacles.

Talk about a cure for fear: God's promises cannot be thwarted by anything. Remember what Paul writes in Romans 8:38–39: "Neither death nor life, nor angels nor principalities nor powers, nor things present nor things to come, nor height nor depth, nor any other created thing, shall be able to separate us from the love of God which is in Christ Jesus our Lord."

That's the best news ever. Nothing, nothing, *nothing* can separate us from the love of God.

Nothing in this world.

Nothing in the past.

Nothing that will happen in the future.

Not even angels or demons can separate us from God's love.

Not even *death*.

So, friends, let's face our fear in the power of God with the confidence, the determination, and the *grit* that come from knowing He will never forsake us. He will uphold us with His strong and righteous right hand. And we can walk forward in unstoppable hope, confident that He will do extraordinary things in our lives.

Unlocking Resilience

1. How can you start serving others? Where have you stopped serving others and need to resume doing so?

2. How can you better trust that God is upholding you?

3. What would cultivating a greater awareness of God's presence look like in your life?

9

THE GIFT OF HOPE

2 TIMOTHY 1:7

We're constantly bombarded with a message— sometimes obvious, often subtle—from a million sources: "Be afraid." Life can start to feel hopeless. Thankfully, God is offering us the gift of hope. And because it comes from God, it isn't just temporary.

If you're a parent, you know that one of life's greatest struggles is figuring out where the heck to hide all the Christmas presents.[1] Sure, you can cram them up high in a closet somewhere or stuff them under the bed or up in the attic, but none of that works for long. The kids are *always* going to find the secret stash.

Our secret stash used to be in the downstairs closet. It was like the opposite of a secret. So Lynn came up with a better solution. She told the kids that Santa had given her a special

---

[1] To be honest with you, I still don't know where my parents hid the Christmas presents growing up.

request. "With *so* many people in the world," she explained to the kids, "Santa was wondering if he could drop off your presents early. It would really help him out."

They had to agree, since no one wants to needlessly end up on Santa's naughty list. My wife's clever plan made it so we could buy presents whenever we wanted and that as long as we wrapped them, they could sit out in plain sight.

I know what you're thinking, and you're right: It wasn't gonna be that easy! Our new solution didn't mean the kids weren't curious. If anything, they were even more curious. So instead of wondering what they were getting for Christmas in the abstract, they were constantly guessing what was in specific boxes. It was a total blast. Annabelle reorganized the gifts almost daily. And she always had these far-out, crazy ideas of what she was getting. "I can tell . . . this one's a baby cow!" "Wait a minute. This is a rocket ship!"[2]

That's one of my favorite things about gifts: the sense of expectancy they create. We can't help but wonder what's inside a gift, right? And if the gift giver knows us really well, we're usually even more curious and excited. Since they've given us amazing presents in the past, our feeling of expectancy increases.

Now, I want to ask a deep, complicated question. A real spiritual head-scratcher. We love receiving gifts, sure, but do we know who the ultimate gift giver is?

God is.

Yeah, I said it. God is the ultimate gift giver! I know you

---

[2] I love our little Annabelle, but pray for us. She is actually the answer to my parents' prayers. You know the one: "I pray you get to raise a child *just like you*!" Well, God heard those prayers . . . and He gave us Annabelle.

might be like, "Oh, come on, Fusco, of course you're going to say that. You're a pastor."

And you're right: Of course I'm going to say that! But that doesn't make it any less true.

Our love of receiving gifts is a reminder that God has always been in the gift-giving business. And what is so great about God's gifts is that He knows what we truly need. Sometimes even *we* don't know what we truly need. Maybe you've looked back on a time in your life—whether it was when you were a little kid or just a few years ago—and thought, *I can't believe I used to want that,* or, *I'm so glad I never got what I asked for.*

I remember when I was younger and my aunt decided to get me a baseball glove. She knew I loved baseball. She knew a glove would be useful. But my sweet aunt didn't know anything about baseball. Bless her heart, she tried. But she got me a mitt for a lefty.[3] Not only that, but she thought she was getting me a catcher's mitt, when it actually was a *first baseman's* mitt.[4] I didn't have the heart to tell her. But the amazing thing is we never experience awkwardness or disappointment with the gifts God gives us, because our heavenly Father always knows exactly what we need.

And I believe that in times of uncertainty, in scary times, there is at least one gift that God wants to give *all* of us: hope. Not just the idea of hope, but the gift of actual, real, life-giving hope that comes from knowing the Lord.

---

[3]   I'm not a lefty.

[4]   I also wasn't a first baseman.

DELIVERED FROM FEAR

"God has not given us a spirit of fear, but of power and of love and of a sound mind."

That's how 2 Timothy 1:7 describes what it's like to be one of God's children. The apostle Paul is writing this to a young man named Timothy. Earlier, in 1 Timothy 1:2, Paul calls Timothy a "son in the faith." Paul has been investing his life in Timothy, mentoring him. By this point, Timothy was struggling a bit in his ministry. He was starting to feel overwhelmed by everything that was going on. We've all been there. That's why Paul writes to encourage him, and it's in that context that he says, "God has not given us a spirit of fear, but of power and of love and of a sound mind."

Right away we see something key in Paul's words: It's impossible to receive some of God's gifts if we are living in fear. He wants to trade our fear for His power, love, and wisdom.

I've said this before, but remember that fear is the natural human response to uncertainty. Fear comes to all of us. And when it confronts us, it can make us feel like no one is there with us in the battle. The real question, then, is what we decide to do with that fear. Or looking at it from another angle, the question is where we think that fear is coming from. Fear is natural, but it isn't one of the gifts God gives us.[5] A spirit of fear is something God *replaces* with His good gifts.

How often in the past month have we felt scared about our circumstances? The past year? How often have we felt

---

[5] I make this important distinction every time I talk about fear. The Bible tells us that the fear of the Lord is the beginning of wisdom (see Proverbs 9:10). We fear God because He is mighty and holy and we are not. Fearing God is not the same as living in a spirit of fear.

gripped by fear or isolated by fear? How often have we made decisions based on the fear we're experiencing?

Friends, a fear-based decision can't be a faith-based decision. God has not given us a spirit of fear but rather a spirit of power and love.

Our fears have even stopped many of us from praying. We've stopped saying, "God, I'm seeking You in the midst of all this. And I believe You are bigger than all of it." Prayer is not about getting our will done in heaven. Looking back at recent events we all experienced, plenty of people prayed for the pandemic to end in 2020.[6] But it didn't. So what happened? Great question. You see, prayer involves linking hands with God to get *His* will done on earth.

I believe that in our current moment, linking hands with God to get His will done on earth is more important than ever. It's what He is longing for us to do. He wants to do a work through His people, people like you and me, in the midst of our fear and hopelessness, but first we need to trust Him and let Him replace the earthly fear that grips our hearts.

A fearful heart is an immobilized heart, and it is from our hearts that our words and actions flow. So you can see the problem.

Psalm 34:4 says, "I sought the LORD, and He heard me, and delivered me from all my fears." That's so powerful! We can't afford to be restrained by fear. Our world can't afford it.

We need our fear to be replaced by faith because God's work of transformation happens when we are walking in the confidence of His strength, love, and wisdom.

---

[6]   Me included!

GOOD NEWS AND BETTER NEWS

So if God has not given us a spirit of fear, what has He given us?

The good news is, replacing our fear with faith is exactly what God promises.

One, two, three . . . eyes on me!

Now that I have your attention,[7] don't miss this! Replacing fear with faith is essential for unlocking our God-given resilience. It sounds simple, and, frankly, it is. For most of us, that probably sounds even better than good news!

And all of us love good news, right? And the better the news, the more we love to hear it. That's probably why if there is bad news *and* good news, we tend to want the bad news first, to get it out of the way. It reminds me of what happened at a gas station on November 21, 2012. I was driving home from church and had the radio on as I pulled into a gas station.[8]

Suddenly the worst news ever came over the speakers: Hostess would no longer be making their iconic Twinkies snack. I felt a deep black pit form in my stomach. *No more Twinkies?* This dystopian thought was unimaginable. It was as if the radio host had calmly announced there would be no more oxygen or sunshine. It was as though God had announced to Moses in the desert that there would be no more

---

[7] Sorry for treating you like my kids, but it works on them. And if you are reading this, it worked on you too!

[8] Usually, I don't listen to the radio much, as there aren't *that* many stations that play avant-garde jazz, but that day I'd forgotten my iPod at home.

manna (i.e., Twinkies . . . think about it) from heaven to feed the Israelites.

My mind went straight to the eighties rock song "Don't Know What You Got (Till It's Gone)" by Cinderella.[9] Why hadn't I bought Twinkies the last time I was at the store? Why didn't I have a stockpile on a shelf in the pantry? Didn't they have a shelf life measured in *decades*?

I was supposed to head home after getting gas, but instead I drove around town to find Twinkies. None at Safeway, none at Fred Meyer, none at the dollar store. I started checking out gas station mini-marts. Meanwhile, Lynn was texting me: *Where are you? You're an hour late.* But I was thinking, *I'm not heading home until I find a box of Twinkies.*

Eventually, I had to give up. People smarter and faster than me had bought up every last box of Twinkies in the city, and the snacks were already selling on eBay for insane prices. I trudged through the front door of our house, totally defeated and depressed.

"So *why* were you trying to find Twinkies?" Lynn asked.

"Because they stopped making them!" I answered, exasperated.

"But . . . like . . . we're just talking about . . . Twinkies, right?" she followed up.

"They're *Twinkies!*" I clarified.

That was a dark day in the Fusco house. Part of me is surprised you're reading this, because it means I survived the

---

[9]   And if you don't know this song, you need to listen to it. It's your classic eighties power ballad. Amazing song and the video has all dudes with great bangs in it. It is sublime!

Twinkiepocalypse of 2012.[10] But here's why I bring up this story. Hearing that Hostess was discontinuing the best snack in the universe was a gut punch—until, that is, I heard the best news in the universe. Only a few agonizing weeks later, Hostess announced that in a few months, they would be bringing Twinkies back! I'd be lying if I said I didn't throw my hands in the air and shout, "Hallelujah!" I felt that good news from my toes to the top of my head and, more important, in my taste buds. And the funny thing was, I couldn't wait to tell other people the news as well. Lynn even faked being excited, because that's how much she loves me.

That's just me and my Twinkie addiction, though. That news wasn't even *news* to most people, let alone amazing news. But do you know what's *actually* some of the best news in the universe? I apologize[11] for what I'm about to do, but if I write the song lyric "I've *got* the *pow*-er!" then you're going to have that 1990 one-hit wonder by Snap! in your head all day.[12]

And that's a good thing! Because if you're in Christ, you absolutely have got the power. Not your own, but the power of the Holy Spirit. God has not given us a spirit of fear, but He *has* given us supernatural power, and that's just about the best news we can imagine. Unfortunately, times of uncertainty are often when we forget that God has already given us the power we need. At the exact moment we need it most, most of us are oblivious to how powerful we really are.

---

[10] Possibly another proof of the Rapture! Let the reader understand.

[11] Not really.

[12] You better be enjoying all these music references. And if you aren't, at least I am.

It's one thing to *say* that we have the power of the Holy Spirit. I get that. Many of us just don't *feel* powerful. We feel uncertain or fearful or hopeless.

And in a certain way, that's totally okay, because on our own, we run out of resources *real* quick. But listen to what Paul writes in 2 Corinthians 12:9: "[God] said to me, 'My grace is sufficient for you, for My strength is made perfect in weakness.' Therefore most gladly I will rather boast in my infirmities, that the power of Christ may rest upon me."

How beautiful is that? It is precisely *in our weakness* that God's strength is made perfect. God doesn't take strong people and make them a little stronger. Instead, He takes weak people—which is all of us!—and makes them perfectly strong. His power roars to life where our human power ends. That's why Paul says he will brag about his weaknesses because that's how he can see the power of Jesus in a new way.

Does this news sound too good to be true? That you have a perfect power living inside you?

It can be true for anyone. It *is* true the moment you say yes to Jesus. The power of the Holy Spirit is a gift that God gives to all who believe. When a person says yes to Jesus, the Spirit of God takes up residence in their life. Right now, while you're reading these words, if you've put your faith and trust in Jesus, then the power of the Holy Spirit is inside you.

That's a gift from God—the same gift that transformed the disciples[13] and, ultimately, the entire world. And it's a renewable resource. In Ephesians 5:18, Paul says, "Do not be drunk with wine, in which is dissipation; but be filled with

---

[13] If you're curious, start by reading the first few chapters of Acts. It's a wild ride!

the Spirit." The really cool thing is, when you dig a little deeper into the original Greek language, what he is saying is actually "Be being filled with the Holy Spirit." He's directing us to ask for and receive a fresh infilling of God's power for living, every day.

And if you aren't a follower of Jesus yet or are far from God, I'm excited that you're reading this and learning about who He is. All you need to do to receive God's power is to say yes to Jesus. He is inviting you to be one of His children. He wants to forgive you and save you. And when you say yes, the power of the Holy Spirit on your inside will change what you do on the outside. God's Spirit living in you will have big-time external results. That's a gift that is as tangible as it is hopeful.

WE LOVE BECAUSE WE ARE LOVED

But why does God want His children to be powered by the Holy Spirit?

Here's why. There's something psychologists call the law of reciprocal affection. If someone loves me, I'll love them back. And if they stop loving me, I'll stop loving back. That's one of the only laws we humans are super good at following.

But it's different with God.

His law of reciprocal affection is that He initiates love, regardless of what we're doing or feeling or believing. Then, as we experience God's love, we want to love Him back.

But it goes a step further. As we experience God's love and love God in return, He says to us, "Now go and love other people with My love." That's the upward-inward-outward movement we talked about in chapter 5, and it's all about love. As Jesus puts it in Matthew 22:37–40, " 'You shall love the LORD your God with all your heart, with all your soul, and with all your mind.' This is the first and great commandment. And the second is like it: 'You shall love your neighbor as yourself.' On these two commandments hang all the Law and the Prophets."

Basically, God has proactively and preemptively chosen to love each one of us. You might want to reread that, because I don't always use ten-dollar words like that. *Proactively and preemptively.*

The Bible puts it this way: "While we were still sinners, Christ died for us" (Romans 5:8). God doesn't wait to love us until we deserve His love. He bestows His love on us always—past, present, and future—no matter who we are or what we've done.

But as I like to say, God loves us as we are, and He loves us too much to leave us that way. The reason God gives us the gift of His love is so it can rule in our lives and can overflow from us. Look at what 1 Peter 4:8 says: "Above all things have fervent love for one another, for 'love will cover a multitude of sins.'" We're told to have fervent love above *all* things.

If we want to live in faith during uncertain times, we have to start with love ruling our lives. And it's worth remembering that this isn't love like we "love" carne asada burritos[14] or our favorite movies. This is God's love. Capital-L Love. Love that changes the world.

That's why we need to spend our time loving people, praying for people, and encouraging people. It's so important that we learn, or relearn, the art of encouraging one another.

---

[14] I do love those, though. Really I just love burritos. With anything inside them.

And there's a reason I say encouragement is an art. Real encouragement isn't a science. People's needs change. And if we want to be encouragers, we need to artfully respond to what—and who—we see around us.

It's so worth it. One kind word can change the trajectory of someone's life. A moment in which you stop and give the gift of your full attention to somebody can be a transformative moment—for both of you.

God has given us both the mandate and the power to love others, and there are myriad ways we can do that. Here's the one constant, though: every way needs to be personal. Real encouragement is always person to person. It's a connection. That doesn't mean we can encourage only people we see face-to-face. In a culture where we have a tendency to tear people down, sometimes a simple note—on paper, on a messaging app, wherever!—is all it takes to make a connection.

"Listen, I believe in you and God believes in you."
"I love you."
"I see that you're growing and working hard."
"Hey, I know you're afraid, but I want you to know that God is for you."
"God loves you and is on your side."
"How can I help you?"
"I'm bringing you a frozen dinner this week."
"Hang in there."
"I just thanked God that I know you."

Whatever shape our encouragement takes, it ought to come as a response to God's love. Fear turns us inward, but God's Spirit gives us the power to turn outward in love.

CHECK YOUR HEAD

We've got to keep our heads. Just as God hasn't given us a spirit of fear, neither has God given us a spirit of drama. When times are uncertain, it's easy to lose our heads. It's easy to freak out, whether at ourselves or at others. But that doesn't help us love anyone—not God, not ourselves, and certainly not others.

Things can get pretty crazy pretty quickly in our minds. And that's why I'm so grateful that God gives us the resources we need to keep our heads. Besides a spirit of power and love, God promises the gift and the power of a sound mind. That image is like a sound foundation for a bridge or a house. If the foundation is sound, the whole structure can be sound. The same goes for us.

The apostle Paul shows us in Romans 12:2 why this is so important: "Do not be conformed to this world, but be transformed by the renewing of your mind, that you may prove what is that good and acceptable and perfect will of God."

Instead of being shaped into the image of the world, by the world, we are to be transformed. And that transformation happens when our minds are renewed in God's presence, by His power. God wants to do a work of renewal in our minds. He wants to give us the mind of Christ. He wants to teach us how to keep and steward and guard our minds in such a way that even in the midst of uncertainty, we have that unstoppable hope.

But God doesn't do brainwashing or mind control. Instead, it's a process of maturing in Christ and growing in His character. He grows us, lovingly, as we relate to Him. As we live life and love others. As we read our Bibles.[15] As we pray.

And it's as we're transformed by the renewing of our minds that our lives begin to demonstrate the good and acceptable and perfect will of God.

It's like that famous line from René Descartes, "I think, therefore I am."[16]

So much of life happens inside our minds. That's what makes it so great that God renews and transforms them. When that happens, we don't just think differently—we live differently. We can breathe again. And we begin to do things that demonstrate, to ourselves *and* to others, the incredible, hope-filled plan God has for us.

DON'T FORGET YOUR GIFTS

There's a certain prayer I try to pray. It's a challenging one, but over and over in my life, I've seen that it's a good one. A powerful one. I pray it whenever there's something going on in my life that I don't enjoy.

"Lord, You know I want You to take this away, but while it's here, will You use it to bear the fruit that You want to bear in my life?"

Even as I am writing this chapter, I am praying that prayer.

---

[15] This is one of the main reasons I encourage people to use a daily or weekly Bible-reading plan. You can pick one up for free at https://crossroadschurch.net. Life can frazzle us, but God is never frazzled! Hearing from Him through His *Word* instead of the *world* is truly transformational.

[16] I had to look up who said this. The only other thing I know about Descartes is that you shouldn't put him before the horse.

Why? Because we just had to say goodbye to our beloved family dog, Molly. Actually, I am not a dog person.[17] My experience with dogs hasn't always been the greatest. I didn't grow up with a dog, except for our neighbor's, who bit me when I was pretty young.

Then as I got older, I found out that I was allergic to dogs. I'm talking about the swollen eyes, stuffy head, coughing kind of allergic. It's not that my parents ever wanted a dog, but my allergies ensured that the Fusco family wouldn't have a dog.

But eleven years ago, the pleas of my wife and (at the time) two little kids totally won me over. I wanted to be a great dad and husband, and I just couldn't say no to those three faces. So they brought home the cutest black Labrador mix. Of course, they all promised that they would be up with her in the middle of the night and take care of her every need. And you already know that rarely ever happened. They also promised to clean up after her. How do you think that went?

But over time, I absolutely fell in love with our crazy dog. Sure, she would lick you to death. And dig holes in the yard. And eat things that no dog should ever eat. But, eventually, she became family and I loved her.

And when we had to say goodbye, it hit me hard. I'm still sad. But it's an opportunity for me to say, "God, bear fruit in my life through this sadness." And I know He will be faithful to do just that.

Looking back at the past few years, I wonder if one of the fruits God wants to bear in our lives is humility. We aren't ever in control, but sometimes we act like we are or pretend we are. But not so much anymore.

---

[17] Don't judge me, please.

Life is fragile and can change in an instant. But unlike our world and our lives, Jesus Christ is the same yesterday, today, and forever. He is exactly the same before and after you lost your job. He is exactly the same before and after your loved one caught Covid-19. He is exactly the same before and after that relationship. Jesus doesn't change, even when elected officials do. And it's on that sure and sound foundation—only on that foundation—that we can build lives defined by faith rather than fear. It's when we are in Christ that we are in the loving power of God.

Now, here's the thing. We all know what it's like to receive a gift and then forget we have it. Maybe it's a gift we don't love. Like if someone gave me a treadmill, I'd say thank you and then look for the darkest corner of my house to hide it in.[18] But it can happen with good things too. What percentage of Starbucks gift cards are spent all the way down to zero before being lost in a drawer?

So if you're reading this right now and you're following Jesus, remember that you already have heavenly gifts! You have a spirit of faith, not fear, and you have power and love and a sound mind. But are your gifts locked away and forgotten?

Now more than ever, we can't afford to ignore the power we have from the Holy Spirit. Sometimes we need to pray to the Lord, "God, please forgive me. I've totally been neglecting the gifts that You have already given me. I feel trapped by fear, but I want to replace that fear with Your good gifts."

God created us to be in Christ. He sent Jesus to earth on a mission to rescue us and empower us. We can't save the

---

[18] And then I'd cover it with a blanket and lock the door to that room.

world, but because Jesus can, we can walk into our families and neighborhoods filled with courage, loved by God, and ready to love others. I can't think of a more hopeful gift than that.

Unlocking Resilience

1. Where do you need to exchange fear for faith?

2. How does God want to bear fruit in your life through your unpleasant or stressful circumstances?

3. Who can you proactively and preemptively show love to?

10

THRIVING IN STRESSFUL SEASONS

Wish we could turn back time to the good old days,
When our momma sang us to sleep, but now we're stressed out.

—Twenty One Pilots, "Stressed Out"

I come from New Jersey, a place where the weak are killed and eaten.[1] But even when I lived in New Jersey, I never met anyone who wanted *more* stress in their life.

---

[1] Don't worry—I'm joking (well, mostly). If you're from there, you know what I mean.

When I'm asked to define stress,[2] I like to say that stress is simply our bodies reacting to change. Whenever something changes, we make adjustments, whether we realize it or not. And it doesn't matter if those adjustments are tiny tweaks or massive—we still need to make them. Whenever we do, that affects our minds, hearts, and spirits. We change because life is changing around us.

And there's the other side of the coin too: the lack of change. The more that things aren't moving in a direction we want or sitting in a place we don't like, the more it stresses us out.

Sometimes we know this is happening, but just as often we're oblivious. Our bodies usually aren't, however.

It's not stress that kills us, it is our reaction to it.

–Hans Selye, *The Stress of Life*

Years ago, I was waking up every morning with a splitting headache and a sore jaw, so I decided to ask my dentist about it.

"You're grinding your teeth when you sleep," my dentist told me. Before I could say anything, she stuck her little mirror back into my mouth to confirm. "I can see the wear on your molars. How's your stress level?"

"Ah a hale ah un oo en," I began. Luckily she took her

---

2   Like when I'm writing chapters about it in a book, just to pick one totally random example.

little mirror out of my mouth. "On a scale of one to ten," I tried again, "my stress level is at eleven." I smiled, hoping she would dig my *This Is Spinal Tap* reference.

"Mine too," she replied seriously. *Clearly not a Christopher Guest fan,* I thought. "Well, let's fit you for a night guard."

And when the hygienist came in, the dentist moved on to the next patient.

If only all our stresses could be resolved with something as simple[3] as a night guard.

Unfortunately, our world is broken in tons of different ways, and as a result, we are *constantly* bumping up against change and pressure that we have to process. Life is so messy that there are actually different types of stress: acute, episodic, and even chronic. We can feel stress over virtually everything because at the end of the day, nothing is certain.[4]

I don't know about you, but recently I feel like my stress levels are back up to eleven. Life has been way beyond what I knew "out of control" could be. And with everything I'm hearing from people I talk to, I wonder how many of us are reaching the breaking point.

So what can we do about it?

First, we trust in the reality that God knows us inside and out (see Psalm 139; Luke 12:7). That's something we can rest in.

Second, that means God wants to do a unique work in our

---

[3]   And handsome and manly and just generally cool.

[4]   Are you wondering about those stress statistics and interested in reading more? Check out this page from the American Institute of Stress: www.stress.org/daily-life.

lives, even in the midst of stress. He knows us *and* our stress, and His Spirit wants to help us move from just "hanging in there" to victory.[5] And believe it or not, we may even find ourselves *thriving* in the midst of stress.

Are you wondering how that's possible?

It's simpler than you might think. However, it's *not* that simple of a sentence, so I like to lay it out like this:

> When we hope in God
> *while* taking resilient steps forward
> *with* grit
> (and drenching everything in hope),
> we unlock God's unstoppable plan
> and we make it!

We are healthier when we internalize this reality: *Stress will be part of life on this side of eternity.* That's the first step.

But we can't reach full health, let alone wholeness, until our hearts go from hopeless to hope-filled. We can't reach full health until we live with grit and determination.

That's when we'll begin to understand that our stressful situations are also God's opportunities.[6] And *that's* when stressful experiences actually make us more like Jesus, which is how God designed us to be.

---

[5] You don't want to be just that cute kitten from the motivational poster, do you?

[6] *Godportunities,* as I like to call them. Catchy, huh? To be honest, I stole the phrase from Crossroads' founding pastor, Dr. Bill Ritchie. But it's mine now!

11

STEADY UNDER STRESS
1 THESSALONIANS 1:2-4

We live in times of uncertainty, and sometimes we can feel completely overwhelmed by it all. Yet Jesus invites us to trust that we are gonna make it. We can walk in a uniquely resilient hope that helps us stay steady under stress.

Questions are a normal part of life.

All of us have certain questions that just rattle around in our heads. Here in the Pacific Northwest, where I live, many people have the same question: Why, at the end of Super Bowl XLIX, did the Seattle Seahawks throw a pass on the goal line instead of handing it off to Marshawn Lynch?[1] This may not be the most important question in the world, but believe me, if you ask it as a conversation starter around here, you'll get an earful.[2]

---

[1] Just mentioning Marshawn makes me hungry for Skittles.

[2] In case you don't know how this game ended, Tom Brady and the New England Patriots once again won the Super Bowl. Had the Seahawks

I remember one time when Annabelle was about five years old and she had a super-important question. She's always been a modern woman who knows what she wants and speaks her mind. And this time, she hopped into Lynn's car after preschool and was in a mood, you know?

"Mom, Holly[3] said that I'm yucky, but I'm not yucky! I just pick my nose, but I'm not yucky! Why can't I pick my nose?"

Lynn was doing her best to drive safely while silently laughing so hard, and she pulled it off. When I got home and heard the story, I went to have a chat with Annabelle.

"Sweetie, what happened?"

She got right to the point. "Dad," she said, "why can't I pick my nose?"

Now, I did *not* want to make this gal mad, so I was like, "Girlfriend, you can pick your nose all you want. Go ahead. Pick away!"[4]

I figured she'd stop picking it on her own, you know? But her question got me thinking: Why *can't* we pick our noses? We blow our noses. We scratch our itches. We rub those little crusty bits out of the corners of our eyes. We even pick our teeth, for goodness' sake. How's that any different from picking our noses?[5]

---

won, it would have been back-to-back Super Bowl victories for them. And they haven't been back since.

[3]   Names have been changed to protect the guilty.

[4]   Pro tip for all the dads out there: What's better at stopping teenage boys from asking out your amazing daughter than her routinely picking her nose in public? I rest my case.

[5]   Dad-joke time: Remember that you can pick your friends and pick your nose, but you can't pick your friend's nose.

All of which is to say, questions aren't even just a normal part of life. Questions are an essential part of life. And when it comes to God, questions are par for the course. He is not scared of *any* questions we may have. We can love the Lord and believe in Him and still have a ton of questions. Or crazy thoughts. Or doubts. And like in any good relationship, God never asks us to swallow our questions or pretend we have answers when we don't.

The same is true for people who don't believe in Jesus at all. When you're a skeptic, questions abound. And God is not scared of those very real questions either.

Wherever you're coming from, I believe that almost every question we have about God is, in addition to being a question, an invitation to go deeper. To grow in wisdom. To gain revelation or clarity or maturity.

That is especially true—and especially needed—every time the unexpected nature of life smacks us in the face. No matter how much planning we do, no matter how much we think and prepare, and *especially* when we think we have it together, life just surprises us and hits us in weird ways.

When life throws us curveballs—a health diagnosis, issues at work, relational distress, a global crisis, or anything else— it's natural to ask questions.

How is this going to work out?
Am I going to be okay?
What will happen to my family?
Can I afford to miss work?
What's going on with my kids?
What does God want from me?

These types of questions really help us unlock resilience when life is a mess and the clouds have moved in overhead. In unexpected, stressful situations, it's so easy to become overwhelmed—by the choices, the distractions, the fears, the uncertainty. You know what, though? There's also a temptation that hides inside those stressful situations, especially for people who are trying to follow Jesus. We understand that God knows what's best for us, but sometimes we get so overwhelmed with seeking His will in a particular instance that it paralyzes our ability to follow His general day-to-day guidance.

For example, what if your boss fires you for something you didn't do? You may not know exactly how to handle that situation, but you can't let it stop you from following God. You have to keep on keeping on, doing what you're *always* supposed to do, even as the details get worked out.

And that's what I want to show you in this chapter: that believe it or not, we can stay steady under stress, no matter what's going on in our lives. It doesn't matter what questions we have. It doesn't even matter if we have answers to those questions.

The only thing that matters is that we're walking with Jesus. And I don't mean that in a simple, trite way. What I'm saying is that Scripture teaches us how to walk with Jesus, and it promises that when we do, we'll have a steady, failproof faith. We just need the grit to keep on walking.

If you know me, you know I've said this a million times, but that doesn't make it any less true: Life is messy, but Jesus is real, and He loves each one of us even in the midst of our messy lives. That's the foundation of everything.

And on that foundation, we can build our lives. We can

walk boldly, especially when life surprises us. We can buckle down and work, especially when we feel like giving up. Why? Because in times of uncertainty, Jesus is still certain. In times of struggle, He is right there with us. He is *always* certain. He is the foundation of our grittiness as children of God. We keep going—we must keep going—because Jesus is unchanging. And He is asking us to walk with Him in specific ways.

PRAYING AND GIVING THANKS

In order to dig into that and understand it better, let's check out 1 Thessalonians 1:2–4: "We give thanks to God always for you all, making mention of you in our prayers, remembering without ceasing your work of faith, labor of love, and patience of hope in our Lord Jesus Christ in the sight of our God and Father, knowing, beloved brethren, your election by God."

The apostle Paul is writing this to a Christian church in Greece. He's met them before, but now they are distant, so he's sending them a letter. And this stuff we're talking about is so important that Paul begins his letter with it.

Now we're going to look closely at the middle part of this passage, but I don't want us to jump there just yet. The first part is easy to skip, but it matters a ton.

I want you to picture the parents of a kid who has gone off to college. While the kid is studying and partying and doing whatever college kids do, what are the parents doing?

Thinking of their kid. Pretty much always.

I remember during my first semester at Rutgers University, my father called and after a few moments of us catching up, he got right to the point: "Daniel, you *will* call your mother one time a week. Even if you have nothing to say." Boom! He wasn't messing around. Even though I was busy and preoccupied, my parents needed to know that I was doing okay, so I started calling once a week. And it's something I still practice to this day.[6]

That's what Paul is saying to the Christians in Thessalonica. He's thanking God for them, both individually and as a church, and he's praying for them as often as he can.[7]

The amazing thing is that we can apply this to our relationships with God as well. God is glad that He created you! He doesn't pray to Himself, of course, but He knows your name and what you're feeling and where you work and what you dream about, and He rejoices.

Another important thing for us to grab in the first part of this scripture is the fact that Paul, in the midst of his busy life, is praying and giving thanks to God. If we want to be steady under stress, we need to do the same thing: give thanks to God, drawing on our unique confidence in times of uncertainty. Think of what would happen if we looked at a stressful situation and said, "This is an opportunity to praise God and pray to Him for other people."

Listen, no matter how much it feels like it, our lives are *not* determined by what's going on around us. (Go back and read that sentence one more time. It's super important.)

God is God.

God is good.

God has a plan.

---

[6]   Dad, if you are reading this and it's Monday, you know I'll call you on my way to work.

[7]   He says *always,* which would be a lot of praying! I think he means that whenever he thinks about them, he prays for them.

And God is in control, just like always, working in the midst of *whatever* is going on around us. That's the context out of which our praise comes. (Isn't that cool?)[8] God is glad He created you, and part of what He created you to do is give thanks and praise.

And this is coming from just a few sentences at the beginning of one book. You have to love how rich the Bible is! So if you really want to grow in hope and grit, it starts with walking in prayer and praise. And don't let this discipline's simplicity fool you either.

Prayer and praise are absolute jet fuel for your soul.

BECAUSE WE ARE SAVED

I'm going to italicize three words in our passage: "We give thanks to God always for you all, making mention of you in our prayers, remembering without ceasing your *work* of faith, *labor* of love, and *patience* of hope in our Lord Jesus Christ in the sight of our God and Father, knowing, beloved brethren, your election by God."

Work, labor, and patience. Those are what Paul is praising these believers for practicing. And here are a few more italics: they're working at *faith,* laboring in *love,* and patient in *hope.* Faith, love, and hope.

If you've read parts of the New Testament before, that will sound very familiar.

Revelation 2:2 says, "I know your works, your labor, your patience." And 1 Corinthians 13:13 tells us, "Now abide faith, hope, love, these three; but the greatest of these is love."

---

[8]   That's rhetorical. It's most definitely cool!

I think when the Holy Spirit repeats something in Scripture, it's because God knows we might be a little bit thickheaded![9]

In these cases, God is inviting us to work, to labor, and to be patient and steadfast, specifically in terms of our faith, love, and hope.

Now, before we dig deeper into these three ideas, there's an important distinction that I don't want us to miss. When Paul says, "We give thanks to God always for you all, making mention of you in our prayers, remembering without ceasing your work of faith, labor of love, and patience of hope in our Lord Jesus Christ," that sounds a lot like he is praising the Christians in that church for *doing* the right things. That's because he is! And doing is indeed important. But many of us have heard the Bible teaches that people are saved by faith, *apart* from doing the right things. That's because we are!

So we need to be careful to distinguish what saves us—putting our faith and trust in the finished work of Jesus—from what God calls us to do once we are saved (i.e., the works of love and grace that we do because we are so blessed to know the Lord and be loved by Him).

James says it this way: "Someone will say, 'You have faith, and I have works.' Show me your faith without your works, and I will show you my faith by my works" (James 2:18).

We don't do the work of faith to *be* saved. We do the work of faith because we *are* saved.

---

[9]   And in my case, it's not a little bit thickheaded. It's a *lot bit* thickheaded.

WORK OF FAITH

That last paragraph isn't an easy one, so let's unpack it a little more.

Believing in Jesus gives us an incredible opportunity. Faith is a powerful thing, but we often forget that. Faith can make waves in the world. It can change hearts and lives and heal communities when we allow Jesus to work through us. And that's why the "hope + grit" formula matters so much. When we are purposeful with applying our faith, our times of stress transform into opportunities to serve. Our uncertainty gives us a platform to share hope. Even the pain we feel becomes power for transformation.

Looking back on the ways God works in His people, I notice His involvement often seems to happen in times of great stress or struggle. Why would that be? One reason is that those times bring our deepest needs out into the open, and God meets us with His limitless resources.

Here's how the apostle Paul puts it to the church in Ephesus: "By grace you have been saved through faith, and that not of yourselves; it is the gift of God, not of works, lest anyone should boast. For we are His workmanship, created in Christ Jesus for good works, which God prepared beforehand that we should walk in them" (Ephesians 2:8–10).

We talked about it earlier: We aren't saved by doing good things. God's grace, through faith in Jesus, is the only way we're saved. But the reality—the cosmic, world-changing reality—is that God has created us, in Christ Jesus, before we were even born, *to do good works*.

That means that right now, exactly as you are reading this,

no matter what your life or your world looks like, God has already planned amazing things for you to do and be part of. He designed you. And He already knows the ways in which your life is masterfully and uniquely created to declare faith, hope, and love. God wants your faith to be lived out loud, in public, for His glory and for the good of others. And the coolest thing is that living like that gives you the most fulfilling life possible.

I'm sure you, like me, have found yourself forgetting the Lord in times of stress and uncertainty. If only it wasn't so easy to do that! When times are tough, all too often we take our eyes off Him.[10] We're like Peter,[11] filled with faith and walking on water toward Jesus, only to take our eyes off our Savior and start to sink into the waves.

Peter knew he should keep his eyes on Jesus. The absurdity of what he was attempting was evidence enough! But Peter, like all of us at one time or another, allowed his fears to overcome his faith. We are standing on water, but when we look around, our faith can fade as worries cloud the horizon. But since we're not trying to walk across stormy water right this minute,[12] we can pause and do some reflection that Peter couldn't. Think about what we're doing when we take our eyes off the God who

> created the universe and everything in it
> gave life to humanity

---

[10] We're just as likely to forget Him when times are good too, because in those times, it can feel like we don't really need Him.

[11] One of my favorite disciples, because he reminds me of me.

[12] Probably.

planned in love to rescue us
saved our souls
loves us for eternity
works all things together for good
never leaves us or forsakes us
hears our prayers
makes our crooked paths straight
provides for us

Yeah, so *that's* either the God we're keeping our eyes on or the God we're forgetting!

There's so much that can obscure our vision of the Lord, but even the simplest things we focus on will distract us. I don't know about you, but I need to keep my focus on God rather than on newsclips or angry online messages. I'm not saying we should bury our heads in the sand. The opposite, in fact. Remember those good works that God prepared for us before we were born? Well, we've got to know where we're needed if we're going to be Jesus to other people. But we have to keep our ultimate focus on Jesus for that work to come alive.

I strongly believe that if Peter had kept his eyes on Jesus, he never would have sunk.

Ask yourself these questions: *How steady are my eyes in times of stress? Am I fixing my gaze on Jesus, or am I looking around at my circumstances?*

I don't always get this right—keeping my eyes on Jesus, that is. But in my heart, I always want to do it. I know I *should* do it. And part of the good works God has for us is simply in encouraging one another to keep our eyes on Jesus so we can walk toward Him, steady in any storm.

LABOR OF LOVE

So we know we should hold on to faith and keep our eyes on Jesus. But how is our faith supposed to work in the world? What does it look like? Almost always in Scripture, and definitely in 1 Thessalonians 1:2–4, it comes down to one word.

Love.

Now, since we're talking about love, we need to make a quick note of the *kind* of love we're talking about. Like from chapter 9, when I said that I love Twinkies. And if you're going, "That's disgusting!" I love that as well, as it just means more Twinkies at the store for me! But without going into a Greek lesson, I can confidently say that is not the kind of love Paul is writing to the Thessalonians about.

Twinkie love is all about me—how I love the sweet taste and the gooey filling and the little sugary energy boost. But the labor of love that Scripture calls us to is not about me; it's all about others. It's self-giving, self-sacrificial love.

Many of us stop at the word *sacrifice*. Sounds scary, but it doesn't have to be.

I remember back at the start of the pandemic, in early 2020, I witnessed self-sacrificial love as I was traveling on an airplane. All you saw on the news was that this crazy new virus was taking over the world and had landed on our shores. We heard that stores across the United States were sold out of hand sanitizer. All of us were uncertain about the meaning of what we were hearing and what we should do about it. We did know we didn't want to get it! So on our airplane, row by row, little communities of kindness began to form. People passed packages of antibacterial wipes from seat to seat. People squirted precious hand sanitizer in one another's hands. They asked where their seatmates were traveling to and if they were safe and if they were worried. Basically, we were looking out for one another *by giving parts of ourselves to one another.*

Time. Attention. Hand sanitizer. Comfort. It seems really simple when you read it. It makes us wonder if those actions even count as self-sacrificial. They do!

When Jesus is talking to His friends on the night of His betrayal, He says, "Greater love has no one than this, than to lay down one's life for his friends" (John 15:13). That's exactly what Jesus was about to do. But that doesn't mean giving your life as a ransom for many is the *only* kind of sacrificial love—it's just the greatest example!

Any kind of love that takes us outside ourselves is powerful. To love self-sacrificially simply means we take time to share ourselves with others. It's not all about us all the time. It's not about our own family unit. We go outside our own lives and our own family into the world around us to minister. Why? Because it's when we go into the world, keeping our eyes on Jesus, that the world can see God's love. Our acts of love, however big or small, testify to the ultimate, perfect love of God. As the famous phrase says, "Not all of us can do great things, but we can do small things with great love."[13]

That's why times of uncertainty and difficulty are the best times to choose to bless others. It takes purpose—the purpose that comes only through hope and grit. And when we

---

[13] This quote is often attributed to Teresa of Calcutta, most commonly known as Mother Teresa.

take those steady steps of faith, we invite others to walk along with us. What they might not know at the time is that we're walking toward our Savior.

The cool thing is that our concern for others mirrors the heart of God. If there's one thing people need to know about who Jesus is, it's that He chose to labor in love for all of us. The whole message of Christianity is that God so loved the world that He gave His only begotten Son, Jesus. That if anyone would believe in Him, no matter where they've come from, no matter what they've done, no matter the circumstances of their life, they would have everlasting life (see John 3:16).

God knew that you were going to be reading this today, just like He prepared good works for you to do, before you were even born. Now more than ever is the time for us to step out in love and help others. When we find a place to help, we don't need to solve everything. We simply need to ask how we can give of ourselves to make the situation a little bit better. Then, however we can show the love of Jesus in that situation, we choose to do it.

So if we are ready to work in faith, the next step is to keep our eyes on Jesus and step out in love.

CONTINUE TO HOPE

I love to connect with people who don't know Jesus, and I also love the church. And since I'm kind of a corny guy sometimes, I lean into the pastor persona[14] and I'm not scared off by stuff that some people would consider churchy

---

[14] I realize that I might be a unique-looking guy, but that guy with funny hair is still a real live pastor!

or even a little cheesy. If something's true, I don't care *how* cheesy it is—I'm gonna embrace it, especially if God can use it!

So I like to define hope this way:

Having
Only
Positive
Expectations

Now, before someone blows a cork over this simplistic definition, let me finesse it a bit for you. The positive expectations that we should have are centered on God's will being done. Period. Hope is not positive thinking. Hope is not that we get whatever we want. Hope is knowing and trusting that God has a plan and that His plan will be done. No matter what.

To have a settled disposition of the heart, you have to *choose* to keep on hoping. Another way to say it is that we need to be patient in hope. It isn't easy to have only positive expectations. The first time something negative happens to us, it often poisons our well of hope. We know something could go wrong, and from there it's only a short step to expecting something negative to happen. Still, we are not only *encouraged* to hope, but we have been *commanded* by God to have hope.

But the concept of hope in the Bible, and in the life of a Christian, is pretty different from the generalized definition of hope our culture has. Don't get me wrong—our culture loves to talk about hope. We hear the word all the time. And I think that's a good thing. Hope is a great thing!

At the same time, hope is not a nebulous feeling of positivity the way that our culture typically uses it. It's more than just good vibes.[15] Hope needs roots and a focus to be the kind of hope God wants us to have.

In Scripture, the concept of hope goes very deep. It all starts with the foundation. Our hope is built on an eternal, unchanging underpinning: the perfect, finished work of Jesus on the cross. We don't try to drum up positive feelings in ourselves or receive them from the universe and call them hope.

It is this hope in Jesus that has led to some of the most provocative work among the most marginalized. We need look no further than at the work of Mother Teresa and the Sisters of Charity. Their sustained impact among the most vulnerable in India shows the power of the hope that is rooted in Jesus.

But we know Jesus! So we hope in the God who created and sustains everything. We hope because we believe that all authority has been given to Jesus in heaven and on earth and that He will always be with us, both now and in eternity. We lean into those facts because they should be the focus of our hearts. It is then that we will truly have only positive expectations.

God is on our side.

We know He's got a plan.

And we know He's going to work even the hardest things together for good.

You might be thinking, *Oh man, I don't know how you can say that right now. Don't you see what's going on?*

---

[15] Although I am always down for good vibes.

Yes, I see what's going on. I'm not going to *list* what's going on, but yes, I'm aware. There's stuff that happens to all of us, there's stuff that happens to only one person, and there's everything in between. Our world is broken, and that pain seeps through the cracks into pretty much everything.

But here's the thing about Christian hope: It can't be undone by a particular situation, no matter how devastating. It can't be undone by all the pain in the world either. Remember, we're living in the middle of the story. Things are going to get worse and go sideways before the beautiful ending. None of us will see the whole story written in our lifetimes, but one day we'll be able to read the whole thing, and it will be the most joyful, glorious, satisfying story ever.

We know that, because God is always a God of restoration and renewal. That means that when He looks at a difficult situation, He always looks for the fruit it will bear. He brings the most extraordinary things out of situations that seem the most hopeless.

And Christian hope assures us that God is working even when we can't see it. Even when we're scared and stressed out. The great hope that God's kids have is that one day we will be able to look back on any situation—and I really mean *any* situation, no matter how dark or difficult—and say, "So *that's* how God was working. *Now* I see what God was doing back then."

But hoping like this is super hard sometimes. It can even feel impossible. So it takes grit piled on top of grit. When hope is married to grit, when our passion for the Lord drives us to stick in there and wait for His purposes to come to fruition, God's plans unfold in unstoppable ways!

Check out what Paul writes in Romans 5:1–5:

> Having been justified by faith, we have peace with
> God through our Lord Jesus Christ, through
> whom also we have access by faith into this grace
> in which we stand, and rejoice in hope of the glory
> of God. And not only that, but we also glory in
> tribulations, knowing that tribulation produces
> perseverance; and perseverance, character; and
> character, hope. Now hope does not disappoint,
> because the love of God has been poured out in
> our hearts by the Holy Spirit who was given to us.

Now, I don't want to be misunderstood when I ask you to focus on these verses. I'm not a cheerleader for tribulations. And neither was Paul. We don't glory in tribulations because we enjoy them. Tribulations aren't fun. They totally stink. That's what makes them tribulations in the first place. However, we do understand that tribulations are both important and transformative in our lives. Tribulations set the trajectory of our lives by producing—only if we're following Jesus, remember—perseverance, character, and hope. And hope does not disappoint.

I love that. I need that. Hope does not disappoint! God knows that each of us is going to have a hard road ahead. Life is messy. But we can make it through the difficult times if we know how to walk in an unstoppable hope.

FAITH, LOVE, AND HOPE

Think for a minute about the final words Jesus said when He was on the cross.

"It is finished."

That's why our hope is absolutely unstoppable. God has

already finished His cosmic work. Sin and death are defeated. When Jesus lived a perfect life, died a sacrificial death, and rose to new life, everything changed forever.

That's the reality we need to keep in mind during the stressful and challenging seasons we experience. It's the story God is inviting us to step into as we do the work of His kingdom. He wants us to work out our faith in the world, labor in self-sacrificial love, and be gritty in hope—an unstoppable hope, even in uncertain times.

I have an encouraging word for you for when you are feeling discouraged and hopeless. No matter what is happening, you can choose faith, love, and hope. And no matter what happens next, you can continue in faith, love, and hope. And no matter what you experience, you can remember that the amazing story of God's people is not finished being written yet.

And neither is the story of your life, whatever chapter you find yourself in.

I don't know about you, but I want to be steady under stress. Each day, I want to choose to have a faith that is failproof. I don't want to be afraid anymore; rather, I want to trust in God's faithfulness. I want to step into the story He is writing and live self-sacrificially.

I know *I* need that kind of love, so that's the kind of love I want to share with others. And I hope you will do the same.

Unlocking Resilience

1. Make a list of the most stressful things in your life right now.

2. How would a fresh infusion of faith, hope, and love transform your current situation?

3. Does hope feel a bit wishy-washy or weak to you? Search for stories of hope in the Bible on the internet. How do the stories you find speak to you?

12

OVERWHELMED NO MORE

PSALM 61

Do you ever feel overwhelmed? There are count-less things that can overwhelm us, every single day. And the more overwhelmed we get, the more we long for shelter and protection, even to the point of seeking refuge in things and people that can't truly provide that for us. The beautiful thing about following Jesus is that He not only offers us comfort when we feel overwhelmed but also enters into what we're experiencing and endures it with us. He shows us how to be overwhelmed no more.

I've got *so* much love for my middle child, Maranatha.[1] She's such a cool person, not to mention beautiful, inside and out. Maranatha is quite possibly the most solid person in our family. She is reliable and resilient. She teaches me a ton, even about parenting, though she is only an early teenager.

---

[1] And *equal* love for my two other children, just in case they read this.

Sometimes when Maranatha has a lot going on in her life, I'll notice that she's talking herself up, building her confidence by pumping herself up and encouraging herself. So I'll walk by and hear her saying things like, "You can do this, Maranatha. God is good. You *got* this, Maranatha."

I love that she does that. Basically, she's preaching the gospel to herself. When she feels overwhelmed, she reminds herself of what she knows to be true in order to make it through. And you know what? It's a biblical habit. It's exactly what happens in the scripture we're going to look at in this chapter. Psalm 61 is one of the psalms King David wrote, and he takes us on a journey from rock bottom to mountaintop.[2]

What does it mean to be overwhelmed no more? Even if our feelings or our life situations threaten to overwhelm us, what strategies can we employ—or better yet, what strategies does God want us to employ—so that we can live unstoppable lives?

We find part of the answer to that in a song that's thousands of years old.[3] In Psalm 61, we meet King David on the verge of being overwhelmed. He's dealing with some really tough issues in his life, and so he cries out to God.

And maybe to him the hard things in his life feel like a flood that is going to cover him or even drown him. I know the stress of life can feel like that to me, which is why I am drawn to the image David uses here: "When my heart is overwhelmed; lead me to the rock that is higher than I" (verse 2).

---

[2]   This is one of the psalms that is performed "on a stringed instrument." So I'm thinking bass and killer vocals. Like Geddy Lee style.

[3]   Don't miss that the Bible invented classic rock!

Now, as you may know, I got a bit of a late start when it came to walking with Jesus and reading God's Word. When I was still a younger Christian, my pastor's wife, Hillary, was in charge of the women's ministry at church, plus she homeschooled three kids and managed the household. I remember one Monday night she was preparing to lead a Bible study the next day. I asked her how she was doing and she said, with admirable honesty for someone in leadership, "I'm feeling overwhelmed. I don't know if I can do this."

But then she followed up with something that's stayed with me: "When my heart is overwhelmed, lead me to the rock that is higher than I."

I nodded, then asked, "So, is that like a song lyric?"

And bless her for not laughing when she answered, "Actually, that's from the Bible." Now, I suppose you could say I was *technically* correct, since Psalm 61 is a song. But Hillary was drawing strength straight from the source: God's Word.

Can't you just picture that image, like a scene from a disaster movie? Like there's a wall of water crashing toward a scientist, and at the last second, just before she's swept away, the hero of the movie pulls her up to safety.

In this life of trials and tribulations, we need to be led higher. As Psalm 40:1–2 puts it,

> I waited patiently for the LORD;
> And He inclined to me,
> And heard my cry.
> He also brought me up out of a horrible pit,

> Out of the miry clay,
> And set my feet upon a rock,
> And established my steps.

We need to be led higher. Up is the only way out.

WHAT WE CAN HANDLE

You've probably heard the biblical saying[4] that God never gives us more than we can handle.

That might sound pretty good if you're feeling strong, like no matter what comes your way, you'll be able to take care of it. And it might even sound okay if you're feeling weak. Like if you're near the end of your strength, at least you know that God won't burden you with anything *too* terrible. Like when you're already beat down, God will give you only tribulation-lite, and then once you're back to full power, He can wallop you with the heavy stuff again.

Now, you can probably tell I'm being a bit sarcastic here, because thinking about life for half a minute reminds us this isn't really true. Sometimes people who are beat down and stressed to the max *do* get more than they can handle. I bet you can remember a time when you got to the end of your rope . . . and then fell. When you were at your lowest point, stuck in the mud, unable to imagine a way out, let alone actually get yourself out.

So here's what the Bible actually teaches:

---

[4]   Just to be totally clear, it's not actually a biblical saying at all! I was totally shocked not to find it in my Bible when I first started hearing and reading it, because somehow I thought it was biblical.

God never gives us more than we can handle. **FALSE**
God never gives us more than *He* can handle. **TRUE**

We were never meant to live with only what we can handle. Scripture is absolutely overflowing with overwhelmed people who call out to God in their moments of need. And God answers. Every. Single. Time. That's the story of God's people living in a sinful world. From Genesis to the present day, life gets crazy, and then God's kids get overwhelmed and call out to their heavenly Father.

Yet one of the greatest tragedies of our day and age is that so many of us are content to live within the realm of what we are comfortable with, what we think we can handle on our own. To put it more spiritually, once again, we're walking by sight rather than by faith (see 2 Corinthians 5:7). This is true spiritually, but it's true in general as well. If we choose to involve ourselves only when we feel comfortable, we'll miss out on new friends, new hobbies, new adventures, and new opportunities. Many times we'll miss out on the absolute best things in life!

Friends, I believe God wants us to live in such a way that we frequently need to pray, like Hillary, "Lord, lead me higher, higher than myself. When my heart is overwhelmed, my heart is not the end of the story. Lord, lead me higher."

I love what the apostle Paul writes in Colossians 3:1: "If then you were raised with Christ, seek those things which are above, where Christ is, sitting at the right hand of God."

Above. Where Christ is. Higher. I think that in these challenging and uncertain times, God is trying to get our attention. He's inviting us to look up, to look higher; to trust that

He can see what we can't; and to let Him lead us through our difficult seasons and situations.

As I write this, I'm thinking about how it relates to my own family. My bride, Lynn, is such an extraordinary person. I always say she is the kindest person I've ever met.[5]

And in our family, we exist in what I like to call crazy happy chaos.[6] Or mostly happy chaos. (Definitely the crazy and chaos part, though.) Some have described me as boisterous, which I think may be a nicer way of saying obnoxious. And then we've got three amazing kids running around. So what I admire about Lynn is that sometimes she simply says, "Listen, this is overwhelming. I just need the Lord." Or she'll say, "I gotta take a couple minutes with Jesus. I'll be right back."

Lynn has learned through walking with the Lord over the years that she needs to be led higher. And here's the key: The peacefulness and kindness she radiates every day isn't produced by her willpower or her ability to overcome every single stressful situation in her life. It's the exact opposite. Lynn knows that the only way to get through the situations she can't handle is to call out to the Lord for help and to trust that He will always deliver.

Oh, and if it isn't obvious by now, let me just put on my pastor hat and say it straight up: When we pray Psalm 61, "Lead me to the rock that is higher than I," it is all about

---

[5]   Besides Jesus. I mean, I have to say Jesus is kinder, but Lynn is *right* there in second place!

[6]   Do you see what I did there? I hope you are crazy happy. I believe that every time we use the word *crazy* or *happy,* we should include the other one. So we are always crazy happy! I say this because of my book *Crazy Happy.*

Jesus. Of course it is! Jesus is the Rock. As the beautiful hymn says so well, "On Christ the solid rock I stand; all other ground is sinking sand." He's the cornerstone of the life of everyone who follows Him, and He's the only lasting rock upon which we can build our lives.

SHELTER IN THE *RIGHT* PLACE

Unfortunately, we know too much about the term *shelter in place.*

Active shooters. Pandemics. Natural disasters.

Sheltering in place is an unpleasant necessity in a world with so much evil in it. And even though our reasons for sheltering in place might not be the same as King David's, the need for a place of safety and security was certainly on his mind. In verses 3 and 4 of Psalm 61, we see David considering the idea of shelter:

> You have been a shelter for me,
> A strong tower from the enemy.
> I will abide in Your tabernacle forever;
> I will trust in the shelter of Your wings.

Now, King David was a warrior, in addition to being a poet and shepherd and murderer and little brother and a bunch of other things. So the first place his mind goes when he thinks of shelter is a military metaphor. When David says that God has been a strong tower, he's thinking of the most secure place a commander could want. With high enough ground and thick enough walls, you're going to be able to withstand almost any assault.

But since David wasn't merely a military man, he extends the metaphor. Or mixes it. Or maybe both/ands it.[7]

God's ability to shelter David is so complete that even the image of a military fortress can't quite capture it. David goes on to say that he will abide in God's tabernacle (literally *tent*) forever and that he will trust in the shelter of God's wings. I love this combination of images. David is helping us see different sides of God.

Sometimes shelter looks like steadfast and mighty protection, like when it's a strong tower. When literal arrows are flying toward you, three feet of rock is what you want between you and your enemies.

Sometimes shelter looks like steady and relational protection, like when it's a tent of worship. When you can't count on any other relationships in your life, you can always count on God.

And sometimes shelter looks like *nurturing* protection, like when it's the underside of a mother bird's wings. Mother birds don't shelter their young forever. A wing is not a nest. Once the danger is past, mother birds get back to the job of teaching their young how to flourish in the world.

What's super cool is that Jesus picks up on this bird imagery in Matthew 23:37: "O Jerusalem, Jerusalem, the one who kills the prophets and stones those who are sent to her! How often I wanted to gather your children together, as a hen gathers her chicks under her wings, but you were not willing!"

Jesus is speaking to the maternal care of God—the same

---

[7] Is that a thing? I think so. And if it isn't, we just made *both/ands it* a thing! Yay! Go, us!

care Jesus shows for each of His children. But whatever the picture of God's shelter, the message is the same: We need to pick the right place to shelter.

What happens for many of us when we're feeling overwhelmed is that we don't choose the right place to shelter. We don't choose the strong tower, the worshipful tent, or the protecting wings. When we try to shelter apart from the presence of God, what we're really doing is setting ourselves up to keep getting hurt. And, ultimately, if we do that, we'll remain overwhelmed.

When I was working through my issues with addictions, I learned that temptation and then pain like to hit us when we're hungry, angry, lonely, tired[8], stressed out, and so on. When our bodies and minds are overwhelmed, we have a tendency to relapse in recovery. We run to the wrong things because they seem easier, only to discover that a moment of ease usually leads to more pain.

What David is teaching us is the biblical version of sheltering in place.[9]

When we're overwhelmed, we need to learn the art of calling on the only One who can help us. We can pray, "God, I want You to lead me higher. I need Your protection. Cover me with Your wings and shelter me in Your strength."

Friends, in my life, I have practically earned a PhD in running toward the wrong shelter. I'm an expert. Before I started

---

[8] I like to remember it with the acronym HALT—Hungry, Angry, Lonely, and Tired.

[9] King David knew how to do that. But if you remember his life, he was far from perfect at it! There were times when David chose to shelter in the wrong place, like with his sin with Bathsheba and the murder of Uriah.

walking with the Lord, I knew *every* wrong shelter. All it took was a little bit of hurt, a little bit of sadness or stress, and I'd race to the closest casual relationship, the closest drug, or the closest shot of tequila to try to find a little comfort or false protection. And even after God started working in my life, I found some other, more respectable versions of the wrong shelter. I'd run to entertainment, the bottom of a pint of Ben and Jerry's ice cream, or the nearest cultural news distractions. These things are cheap substitutes for real shelter, and they can't truly protect us, yet we still flee there to try to find some sort of pacifier.

The truth is, though, that anything less than our Rock can never satisfy, protect, or comfort us. When we realize that, we take a major step toward persevering through our difficulties, because in turning away from the counterfeits that distract or numb us, *we are choosing hope.* Resilient hope. Hope that will not leave us empty or ashamed.

WHERE IS OUR FOCUS?
So . . .

Wanting to be led higher? *Check.*

Sheltering in the right place? *Check.*

But there's one more step: We have to focus and keep Jesus in the center of our minds and our lives. Let's look at what David writes in verses 5–7 of Psalm 61:

> You, O God, have heard my vows;
> You have given me the heritage of those who fear Your
>   name.
> You will prolong the king's life,
> His years as many generations.

He shall abide before God forever.
Oh, prepare mercy and truth, which may preserve
him!

Focusing on one thing changes the way we see *other* things.

Have you ever been outside on a starry night and noticed a particular star out of the corner of your eye? Then when you look straight at it—*poof*—it disappears? That's because our eyes have two main types of cells: cones and rods. The cone cells in the center of our eyes work better at seeing colors, and the rod cells, which are off-center, work better at seeing light and dark. Stargazers learn to look sort of sideways at certain stars, which lets the right cells in their eyes do their job.

Life is like that. We've got to focus the right way. The problems of life can absolutely scream for our attention, but it isn't until we focus on Jesus that we have any prayer of figuring out those problems.

Part of the reason we find it so hard to keep our focus on Jesus goes back to fear. Like Peter walking across the water toward Jesus (see Matthew 14:28–29), we get overwhelmed by everything that could go wrong and all the things we can't handle. But we must remember that it isn't up to us to handle everything! If we doubt that God can handle a situation in our lives, we'll absolutely get overwhelmed. If we feel like maybe He's got a limited capacity within our lives, then yeah, panic and fear are understandable reactions. But what we see so beautifully in Psalm 61 is that God will keep us in perfect peace as we focus on Him, as we *trust* in Him.

Another reason we find it hard to focus on Jesus is our

false sense of our true identity. Over the years, this has become crystal clear to me. If I don't find my identity in the finished work of Jesus, I'll find something or someone else to give me a sense of identity. And the hardest part is that some of these less-than-God identities are, in and of themselves, good things!

This problem doesn't have to be some dramatic moral scale, with God on one side and Satan on the other: *Hmm, should I find my identity in God or in the devil?* Rather, it plays out in subtler ways. For a pastor like me, it happens if I think too much about the effectiveness of the ministry that I'm doing. Effective ministry is a good thing, but it can also draw my focus away from Christ.

It could be almost anything that distracts us from keeping Jesus at the center. It could be our kids' health or grades. It could be our perceptions of the strength of our marriage. It could be trying to get into the college of our choice. It could be trying to find the right person to start a family with. It could be our desire for success. The list is endless.

All these things can form identities for us that aren't ultimate and thus can't last.

To grow in resilient, gritty hope, we need to take a step back from any lesser, insufficient identities and confess the truth that our lives are hidden in Christ Jesus (our Rock, remember?), and His finished work on the cross is all that we need. God is inviting us to live in the reality of who we really are. Or maybe it's better to say that He is inviting us to *see* the reality of who we really are, because our true identity can't change. All we can do is finally focus on it.

In Psalm 61, David has his eyes lifted up to the Lord. He's being led higher, he's sheltering in the right place, and now as he keeps his eyes on the Lord, his whole perspective on life is beginning to change.

Who do you know that lives like that? For me it's my grandma Anita. The other day, I was video chatting with her. One thing I love about her is that she totally embraces technology like that, even though it's like a blip in the scope of the ninety-six years she's been walking this earth. Her attitude is that if a newfangled screen helps her stay in touch with her favorite grandchild,[10] she's all for it. So I'll dial her up and sometimes she won't know where her glasses are, and she'll hold her smartphone *way* too close to her face. Pretty much all I see on my end is one of her eyeballs, you know? But I love it!

So the other day I asked her, "Grandma, how you doing?"

And she was like, "I'm doing pretty well, thank God."

After I gave her an "amen," she said, "I do miss your grandpa, but I'm doing good. I'm here today, and I'm so happy to talk to you. Now, Daniel, how are all the sweeties doing?"

Since those "sweeties" are my kids, I happily gave her a rundown of what they were all up to. But after the call was over, I reflected on how her focus was in the right place. She and my grandpa had been married for seventy years! So her soul mate is already in heaven, and she's stuck on this side of eternity with every right to be bitter or lazy or selfish or whatever. But instead she's grateful to God and focused on loving and encouraging others.

That's the definition of getting your focus in the right

---

[10] She doesn't say that, but I will, just so my sisters and cousins know who is Grandma's favorite.

place. Grandma Anita sees herself in Christ. She knows she's not going to live one day longer than God has planned for her. And in the meantime, she's letting Him keep her in perfect peace, even in the midst of overwhelming things happening around her. She's choosing to trust. By choosing to focus on the right things, she's choosing to hope.

And she, like David in Psalm 61, shall abide before God forever.

RESPONDING IN DAILY LIFE

Notice two simple *p*-words (*praise* and *perform*) in our final verse:

> I will sing praise to Your name forever,
> That I may daily perform my vows. (Psalm 61:8)

Now, I don't love the connotations of the word *perform* in this translation. *Perform* makes it seem like someone putting on a show. But basically what David is doing here is executing what he's learned about how not to be overwhelmed. So we're going to go with *praise* and *practice*.

If you want to live a resilient and hope-drenched life, you need to keep doing what you know to be right, no matter what. Praise and practice. No matter what.

David has his heart and mind on eternity, and he realizes that although he may be overwhelmed in a certain moment, he's being led higher, he's sheltering in the right place, and he's got his focus on the Lord. That reality is what allows him to basically say, "God, You are so good that all of eternity isn't enough time to praise You, and my entire life isn't enough time to walk in the ways You're preparing for me."

Praise and *practice*. Those two words tie this entire Psalm together, just like they remind us—now—how not to be overwhelmed. They are also powerful opportunities to truly live the unstoppable life: a life characterized by hope and grit.

Whatever praise we give God on this side of eternity, it's only going to be better and more extravagant in the hereafter. In this life, we see and know only partially, but in heaven, we are going to know God perfectly, as we are known by Him. That's why choosing to praise the Lord even when we feel as though life is beating us down is a game changer. We can put on a worship song or stretch our hands to the heavens or pray in our cars while we're stuck in traffic. The important thing is that praising God in the storms of life completely changes how we feel. Why? Because in the greatness of His majesty, our present issues start to look a lot different.

In my life, the feelings of being overwhelmed come pretty often. This was heightened as we journeyed through the rough years of 2020 to 2021. We were asking questions that felt disorienting:

> *How will we manage to homeschool our three kids for a year?*
> *What's going to happen with our loved ones who are vulnerable?*
> *How should I pastor a church that can't meet in person because of a pandemic?*
> *Is life ever going to return to normal?*

So what about you? If you're overwhelmed because your job is stressful and hard, can you praise God for that job—

and your boss? Maybe you're overwhelmed because of everything going on with your family right now, but in the midst of that, can you praise God for them? Maybe the polarized political climate makes your blood boil, but are you choosing to focus on the Lord so anger doesn't find a home in your heart? Whether your problems are on the smaller end or are of the life-changing kind, the principle is the same.

King David reminds us that all praise leads to practice. Godly actions are the natural outcome when we are led higher, shelter in the *right* place, and keep our focus on the Lord. Reading the Bible, praying, serving our families and our neighbors, confessing our sins, worshipping, giving financially to God's work in the world—all those practices flow from a right relationship with God.

Remember, we don't believe that God saves us because of the things we do. But because we're saved, we want to live differently. I serve the Lord, not so God will accept me but because He has *already* accepted me. I read Scripture, not so I can earn God's approval but because Jesus said, "Man shall not live by bread alone, but by every word that proceeds from the mouth of God" (Matthew 4:4). And I want to eat God's Word the way I eat my favorite food![11] Let's try praying like this:

> *Lord, lead us to the rock that is higher. When we feel overwhelmed, shelter us with Your love and provision and protection. Keep our focus on You, that we may praise You all of our days. And help*

---

[11] And you know Twinkies are my favorite food. Don't judge me!

*us walk all of this out, daily, as we simply respond
to what You have done for us.*

God wants us to shelter in His protection no matter if our problems are tiny, huge, or in between. He wants to be that strong tower for us when our enemies are near. He wants us to abide in His tabernacle—in His Son, Jesus. And He wants us to praise Him and practice, every single day, so that we might grow deeper and closer to who He is.

Unlocking Resilience

1. Memorize Psalm 61:2.

2. Can you think of a time you praised God in the midst of something difficult? What happened?

3. Ask a friend to tell you about a time God sheltered and protected them.

4. Choose to praise God when you feel like complaining about your overwhelming situations.

13

SETTLED AND RESILIENT

PSALM 27

It's natural to want life to be a smooth, easy stroll. But life is full of hills, valleys, and rocky paths. The journey is often a jagged one, and on our own we can't have genuine confidence we'll make it. That's why Jesus wants us to walk in settled confidence no matter where we find ourselves.

Our culture *loves* confident people.

Self-assured politicians always claim to know the right answer. Athletes always believe they're going to win the game. And there's a steady stream of poised singers who think they can beat the rest of the TV talent-show contestants. But few people can match the confidence of a ridiculously good-looking male model.

I bring this up because of this one time Lynn and the kids and I were chilling on the beach. It was a perfect day—seventy-five degrees, sunny, a light breeze—and we were just goofing off like families do. We tossed the football around, enjoyed our slightly soggy sandwiches that had too much sand in them, built sandcastles, took a few smiling family selfies, and generally found our happy places.

All of a sudden we saw these two guys who just didn't look like they belonged on the beach. The first guy *maybe* could have passed for a beachgoer. He was wearing camo pants and a tie-dye shirt . . . but then the effect was ruined by his oversized new Timberland boots. Not to mention he was carrying a tripod and a camera.

Which explained the second guy's appearance. He was wearing the nicest pinstripe suit I've ever seen. Like walk-down-the-catwalk nice. And, of course, he had on fancy leather shoes.

My son, Obadiah, was like, "Dad, what's that guy doing?"

I just shook my head because I had absolutely no idea. They walked closer to us—the first guy walking like a semi-normal person, the second guy sort of prancing gingerly in his expensive shoes—and we realized they were doing a shoot for an advertisement with the ocean as a background. Camera guy set up his tripod, and suit guy pulled out a leather handbag and started posing with it. Behind his head: *click*. Under his arm: *click*. Pulling a pair of gaudy green shades out of it: *click*. Camera guy was loving the shots he was getting, and suit guy was totally working the camera like he was the only thing that mattered for miles.

That's when Obadiah looked over at me and said, "Dad, wouldn't it be awesome if that dude got hit by a wave?"

I grinned. There are certain moments in a father's life when you just know your kid is on the right track. Not that we wanted them to get hurt or anything. But it would have made for a hilarious moment.

And Obadiah wasn't crazy for thinking about that either.

The waves had been getting higher and higher; plus, the tide was coming in. Maybe it *could* actually happen. So we started joking about it. And before long, Obadiah was praying in King James language. He was like, "Oh, Lord, if it be Thy will, bringest a great wave and smite that dude, in Jesus's name, amen."

I didn't really want to unpack the theology of whether it was appropriate to pray for a wave to hit someone, but I did remind my son that Jesus answers prayers. And Obadiah was like, "Oh, I know."

And sure enough, a minute later, just as camera guy was getting a nice close-up of suit guy, the biggest wave of the day burst onto the beach. Camera guy saw it first, and when he turned to run, suit guy figured out what was happening. He started absolutely jamming away from the wave. I mean, this guy was generating Usain Bolt–level speed in a pinstripe suit.[1] And luckily for him and his suit and his leather dress shoes and possibly his modeling career, he stayed about two feet in front of the wave until he reached safe ground. Obadiah was bummed the wave had missed but stoked he'd seen the whole thing happen.

I bet the suit guy's confidence reminds you of a few people you know. One of the greatest (and most common) human calamities is having inordinate confidence in ourselves. Like the guy in the pinstripe suit on the beach, we forget that there are things outside our control. Sometimes *way* outside our control. So we live that way, assuming so many things will go our way, even though that isn't guaranteed. And what the

---

[1]   Until that moment, I had no clue that leather dress shoes are the best running shoes.

Lord really wants is for us to walk boldly—not because we're confident in ourselves and our circumstances but because we're confident in Him.

I experienced this about twenty years ago when God was gracious enough to help me walk boldly toward my first church plant, at only twenty-four years old. At the time, I was living in California, and I was going to move across the country to start a church in New Brunswick, New Jersey. My native state. The place where I went to college. It just seemed perfect. Thinking back, I'd describe myself as beautifully reckless. I didn't even raise any financial support! I was like, "Dude, I got me, my Bible, the Holy Spirit, and the finished work of Jesus. We're good to go!"

After our church's first meeting (which only a dozen people attended), the offering was less than twenty bucks! At that rate, we wouldn't even be able to pay the rental fees for the space we were using, let alone any other expenses. That's when I first said to myself, *Man, this is not gonna work.*

Except deep down I didn't *truly* think that because I knew God was calling me to that work. My confidence didn't have to be in myself. And He moved in some amazing ways at that church in New Brunswick. It took some time, but it became a vibrant church. Sure, it took a lot of work. And I made a lot of mistakes. But over time, God built something truly beautiful.

Our confidence can take us to places we never thought it could. And when it comes to following Jesus, it's all about where we put our confidence. Who are we confident in?

The Lord wants His kids to have a settled confidence in Him. But it's definitely not easy in all the different situations we face. When times are anxious or our hearts are filled with worry, when we have no idea how things will work out, having a settled assurance that God is in control can be hard.

But having a settled confidence *is* possible, even in the toughest situations life throws at us.

CURE FOR FEAR

So what does it actually look like to have a settled confidence in the Lord? And how do we establish it? The first three verses of Psalm 27 give us a good place to start:

> The LORD is my light and my salvation;
> Whom shall I fear?
> The LORD is the strength of my life;
> Of whom shall I be afraid?
> When the wicked came against me
> To eat up my flesh,
> My enemies and foes,
> They stumbled and fell.
> Though an army may encamp against me,
> My heart shall not fear;
> Though war may rise against me,
> In this I will be confident.

The Lord is our light, salvation, and strength. In dark times, when we don't know the way—even when we feel like it's us against the world and the world is winning—the Lord will show us the path.

The New Testament gives us even more details about this imagery. In John 8:12, Jesus Himself announces that He is the light of the entire world. What could that even mean?

First and foremost, light illuminates. Imagine walking into a dark house and when you flip on the light,[2] you see everything in the room and know where to walk. That is what the Lord does in our lives. He brings illumination and gives us real hope.

And not only is God our light—which, in our dark world, is amazing—but He's our salvation as well. Blessing upon blessing! The name *Jesus* literally means this: God is our salvation. We cannot be saved apart from the perfect work of Jesus, but once we are saved, no one—and nothing—can snatch us from God's hand.

Which is why God is our strength. The One who leads us and saves us is the same One who strengthens us. David, as a great warrior, knew what it was like to be attacked from all sides. He also knew, even as he commanded armies, that his only true strength resided in the power of God.

Check out the questions David is asking in Psalm 27: *Whom shall I fear? Of whom shall I be afraid?* These are important for us to ask as well, and they're not totally rhetorical either. In these uncertain times, there are many reasons for us to be afraid. Too often, we hold those fears in our hearts, but we need to get comfortable introducing our fears to God. We need to introduce our fears to Jesus. Like, "Hey, fear . . . lemme introduce you to my Savior, Jesus. Not to brag, but He conquered fear and death."

See, Jesus is the cure for our fear.

Whatever we're worried about, He is our light, our salva-

---

[2]   Or clap your hands twice if you bought the Clapper from late-night TV ads.

tion, and our strength. If you have your Bible or Bible app nearby as you're reading this, highlight the verses from this psalm. The next time you're nervous or anxious or fearful, remind yourself that God is always on your side. The work of your salvation is finished! If God can save sinners like you and me and call us His own children, nothing in front of us is too big for Him to handle.

That's where we start to get a settled confidence in the Lord: when we introduce our fears to God and claim the promises of Scripture to drive out the fear in our lives.

BE LIKE A TREE

Let's switch up our imagery a bit (and skip back a couple dozen psalms) in order to see even more clearly the provision and protection of God in troubled times. Settled confidence looks like a lack of fear, even when we're surrounded by enemies. And it *also* looks like a healthy, flourishing tree.

Psalm 1, which is one of the most beautiful songs ever written, gives us this image. Check out the first three verses:

> Blessed is the man
> Who walks not in the counsel of the ungodly,
> Nor stands in the path of sinners,
> Nor sits in the seat of the scornful;
> But his delight is in the law of the LORD,
> And in His law he meditates day and night.
> He shall be like a tree
> Planted by the rivers of water,
> That brings forth its fruit in its season,
> Whose leaf also shall not wither;
> And whatever he does shall prosper.

Don't you want to be that flourishing tree? I know I do! That tree has everything it needs to blossom and bear fruit. In other words, it's well rooted. That's what God wants for us as well. It's how He describes a blessed person. Settled confidence means we remain rooted in God and in the finished work of Jesus. When we do that, we'll be fruitful in the ways God wants us to be fruitful, no matter what's happening around us. The tree in Psalm 1 can withstand cold nights and hot days. It can endure seasons of drought. Why? Because its roots go down deep.

Do ours?

And don't think this promise of fruit is only an Old Testament image. Here's what Jesus says in John 15:4–5:

> Abide in Me, and I in you. As the branch cannot bear fruit of itself, unless it abides in the vine, neither can you, unless you abide in Me.
>
> I am the vine, you are the branches. He who abides in Me, and I in him, bears much fruit; for without Me you can do nothing.

God is always glorified when we choose to stay rooted, especially in times of high anxiety, uncertainty, and fear. It's as if Jesus is saying to us, "I want you to stay rooted in Me because I want you to be healthy and confident. You're going to bear fruit, and it's going to be amazing! Live with a settled confidence in Me—in who I am and what I've done."

And that is how grit is cultivated too. Instead of living with flashes of hope and momentary confidence, we allow those roots to gain a deeper hold on the Lord. And we receive more of His nourishing living water and find a stronger footing so in our cold nights and hot days—our challenging seasons of life—we will produce fruit just like that tree with the deep roots.

That's exactly what we find King David talking about in Psalm 27:4–5:

> One thing I have desired of the LORD,
> That will I seek:
> That I may dwell in the house of the LORD
> All the days of my life,
> To behold the beauty of the LORD,
> And to inquire in His temple.
> For in the time of trouble
> He shall hide me in His pavilion;
> In the secret place of His tabernacle
> He shall hide me;
> He shall set me high upon a rock.

David had so many gnarly things going on in his life. One aspect we don't always appreciate about him is that he lived in very violent times. Like D-Day-level violent, on the regular. Every day was a new fight for survival. His subjects even sang catchy songs about how many thousands of enemies he could kill![3]

Yet even with all that going on around him, David has a very singular desire: to dwell in the house of the Lord. Every

---

[3]   Not to mention how many foreskins he collected. Seriously. If that is shocking to us, it's because we are aren't reading our Bibles enough. Scripture is just wild. I look up to King David in many ways, but I never, ever want someone to sing a song about me collecting foreskins.

day, every moment, to live with a settled confidence in God's provision. To have an intimacy with God that transforms his everyday reality.

I realize each one of us is on a journey, and we're all at different stages. Some of us aren't dwelling in God's house. We aren't rooted. We're afraid. And if that's you right now, remember that God is always calling you. He's always asking you to seek His face. He can't wait for you to experience the good fruit that your life will bear when you abide in Him!

SEEK, AND THEN BE FOUND

If I could write this in a bigger font, I would. It's so important. No matter where you are on your faith journey—whether you've been walking with Jesus since before you can remember or you're not sure you believe Jesus is who He says He is—God is saying to all of us, "Seek My face."

That might sound strange to our modern ears. What does it mean to seek someone's face anyway? Basically, it means presence. Access. Intimacy. David is committed to getting close to God no matter what it takes. Why? Because he knows that God is his light, salvation, and strength; because he knows he needs to remain rooted in the Lord; and because he knows God is a good God.

Here's what David says in verses 6–8 of Psalm 27:

> Now my head shall be lifted up above my enemies all
>   around me;
> Therefore I will offer sacrifices of joy in His tabernacle;
> I will sing, yes, I will sing praises to the LORD.

Hear, O LORD, when I cry with my voice!
Have mercy also upon me, and answer me.
When You said, "Seek My face,"
My heart said to You, "Your face, LORD, I will seek."

The truth is, as Ecclesiastes 3:11 says, that God has placed eternity in our hearts. And so I encourage all of us to simply respond to the most eternal and pure part of life, which is God's invitation to an intimate relationship. He *wants* us to know who He is! The one thing He won't do is force Himself on us, because that is not in His character. We're not meant to be God's robots; we're meant to be in relationship with Him.

God created you. He loves you. He sustains you. He has numbered every single hair on your head.[4] God knows not only every interaction you've ever had with another person but also every *motivation* behind every interaction you've ever had. And He is saying, "I want you to know that I see you and I know you. Seek Me."

All it takes is a single honest sentence: "God, I want to seek You and know You."

That's it!

As I look back on my own journey, I'm so grateful to God. I didn't grow up following Jesus or reading the Bible or wanting to serve the Lord. I didn't think about honoring God each day. But there was one thing I did right: When I figured out that God wanted me to know Him, I responded. Simply, maybe even naïvely, but I responded. I was like,

---

[4] For those of you without hair, I have a good word: He loves you too!

"So God wants me to know Him? *God* wants to be in a relationship . . . with me? All right, I'm going to take the next step."

And here's the cool thing: God isn't an absentee landlord. He didn't create the world and then vanish to some far-removed heaven. He didn't create us in order to turn His back on us. Listen to what God's Word says in Acts 17:26–28:

> He has made from one blood every nation of men
> to dwell on all the face of the earth, and has deter-
> mined their preappointed times and the boundar-
> ies of their dwellings, so that they should seek the
> Lord, in the hope that they might grope for Him
> and find Him, though He is not far from each one
> of us; for in Him we live and move and have our
> being.

Think about the why in that verse. Why did God create every single human in all of history? So that they should seek the Lord and discover Him!

Seeking God is a lifelong journey for the believer. Because we're finite beings, part of the way we search for an infinite God is to grope for Him. The picture is that we're in the dark, reaching out, just hoping to find what we're searching for. And Scripture is so beautiful here, because even as we search in the darkness, God is not far from each one of us.

Sometimes that isn't easy to believe, depending on your personal experiences. Have your parents forsaken you? Have you been abandoned by people who are important to you? Were you hurt or abused by the people meant to protect you and provide for you?[5]

Hear this word: *God will be your family.* Even if everyone else in your life deserts or even detests you, God will never leave you or forsake you. David puts it this way in Psalm 27:10: "When my father and my mother forsake me, then the LORD will take care of me."

God will do a work of redemption because He loves you like a perfect Father, a holy Father, a gentle Father. Your life with Him isn't a cosmic version of *Where's Waldo?* God wants us to seek *and* find Him. God wants us to know Him, even as we are known. And as we grow in the knowledge of our Lord, we bear fruit in our lives.

Peace instead of fear. Goodness instead of bitterness. Faithfulness instead of anxiety.

HOPE BIRTHS COURAGE

Maybe that sounds a little too . . . I don't know . . . spiritual? Or too hard to pull off in real life? Or maybe you have tried but haven't experienced what I'm describing? Well, I've got good news for you: David wondered the exact same thing. Check out what he writes in the rest of Psalm 27, picking up at verse 11:

---

[5]   If you are answering yes to any of those questions, I am truly sorry. The thought of that is just heartbreaking, and I cannot fathom the experience of it. Can I gently encourage you to seek help from a trained professional? Also, God's grace is essential for helping you find wholeness. God wants you to grow in that grace every day, even in your pain. Please know that I am praying for you.

Teach me Your way, O LORD,
And lead me in a smooth path, because of my ene-
    mies.
Do not deliver me to the will of my adversaries;
For false witnesses have risen against me,
And such as breathe out violence.
I would have lost heart, unless I had believed
That I would see the goodness of the LORD
In the land of the living.

Wait on the LORD;
Be of good courage,
And He shall strengthen your heart;
Wait, I say, on the LORD! (verses 11–14)

Did you see that? Even King David would have lost heart . . . *unless* he believed God was good.

And that doesn't just happen, right? Believing that God is good is not an involuntary reflex for most of us. It's not like we get a cancer diagnosis or get served with court papers or get an unexpected bill in the mail and immediately say, "No worries—God's got this!" and then go make a sandwich.

No, having a hope that "does not disappoint" takes patience and perseverance. Stick-to-it-iveness. In other words, *grit*.

Check out how David defines it. Wait on God: in faith, with hope. Have courage. And God *will* show up.

That's so powerful. And we need to hold on to it tightly.

I feel like I know verses 13 and 14 inside and out, because I've lived them so many times. They are what I like to call "life verses" for me. They help me realize that any mess I find myself in is an opportunity to grow, to learn, to trust, and to encourage hope to rise up in my heart. When I pray these verses, as I have so many times, I find that I can walk forward in courage, knowing that God will strengthen me even as I'm uncertain or fearful. It's not an instant fix for my situation. But by God's grace, it's an instant fix for *me* in my situation.

I believe that many of us need to hear this message right now. There are so many reasons to be afraid. If you're reading this, you probably don't have literal armies coming against you like David did.[6] You *might* have people falsely accusing you and breathing threats against you. Or it could be a million other things. I know you've got your own list of adversaries and adversities. All of us do. The details change, but the sense of fear is the same.

That's the context in which David reminds us not to lose heart. To believe we will see the goodness of the Lord in our situation. To rest in a settled confidence that the Lord, who is our light and salvation, will be our strength. It's amazing that that powerful, protective God is also the God who invites us to seek His face and pray in friendship and confidence every day.

And the beautiful thing about this intimacy with God is that it's a two-way street. As we live with hope and press into the Lord and His will with grit, He reminds us of who He is and what He brings to the picture.

It's as if the Lord is saying to us,

---

[6] Probably? I mean, I guess there *might* be a reader or two with literal armies coming against them. In which case, I'm glad you're reading this!

You can rest easy, My child.
Everything will be okay.
While you sleep, I am watching over you.
I created you with a plan and purpose.
And I will take care of you.
My mercies are new every morning.
And I will be faithful.

Where else can we find such hope?
Nowhere.

When we place our hope in God, it births courage in us. That's so cool that I'm going to say it again. Hope births the courage we need to face adversity and fear. If God is for us, who can be against us? We've got this. Or better yet, God's got this!

I know not all of you believe in Jesus, but at some level, you're drawing closer to Him even by reading this book. And I want to testify from my own life that it's so awesome to know Him. I'm filled with gratitude for the perfect life and finished work of Jesus. I'm filled with gratitude that God is my Father and that the Holy Spirit has sealed my life.

Nothing has changed my life like knowing God.

Which is why every time He says, "Come on, get to know Me!" I want to take Him up on His invitation. God is inviting you too. Say yes!

Unlocking Resilience

1. Do you have a life verse or verses? Memorize those important scriptures.

2. What steps can you take to live a more "rooted" life in Jesus?

3. What was the last major "bump" on your journey?

4. How can you seek God's face in fresh ways?

14

YOU CAN DO THIS

One of the hardest things about life is the constant uncertainty about what will happen in the future.

It's also one of the most beautiful.

Recently, my wife and I had the pleasure of joining some friends on their wedding day. It's always such a stunning experience when a couple stands before the Lord, before their family and friends, and makes a covenant commitment to be married. This couple wrote their own vows, and as we listened to them make promises to each other, one thing that shone through was that no matter what happened in their lives, at least they would be doing it together. But that is the beauty of the wedding day. No couple actually knows what will happen on their journey. How will each of them grow? What struggles will ensue? How challenging will it be? There's something so real about that in the midst of uncertainty.

Marriage isn't the only source of uncertainty, is it? We change jobs or move apartments or wonder about our health and, well, generally everything!

Like what about having kids? I was laughing the other day while I was talking to a friend of mine. He's been married for a while, and he and his wife haven't had kids yet. So when he was like, "I wonder what it's gonna be like when we have kids," I had to open my big mouth.[1]

So I started to mess with him. "You know all those fun things you and your wife do now?"

He nodded and smiled.

"Well," I kept going, "you're not going to do any of that."

I could tell from his face he was reconsidering the whole becoming-a-dad idea, which made me laugh even harder.

A few days later, I was working from home and ended up on a quick video chat with the same friend. All of a sudden Annabelle, who was three years old at the time, came into my office and was sucking on one of those lollipops that turn your tongue and teeth and lips a freaky shade of blue. She trotted right over and sat on her daddy's lap and looked at the computer screen. Then she did what any little kid does in that situation: She ignored my friend and stared at herself. Or more specifically, at her blue tongue and teeth and lips! She started making the weirdest faces she could imagine, and I began to laugh because my friend's face was processing a lot of emotions.

"Bro, this is what having kids is all about right here!" I said sagely, pointing at Annabelle.

He looked as though he'd just swallowed a fish,[2] which I assumed meant that he was now fully on board with becoming a dad.

---

[1]   What's the point of having three kids if you can't be the kid expert around your kid-less friends?

[2]   I'm talking about a whole nasty fish, not some sort of swanky sushi roll.

In that moment, I was continuing our joke, sure, but also I wasn't. I was serious, and if you have kids, you know exactly what I mean. The beauty is that we don't know what's going to happen. Life is full of tremendous amounts of uncertainty. Sometimes it's a surprise visit from a blue-mouthed girl. Other times it's something heavier or darker. But at the same time, not everything about the future is uncertain. Lots of uncertainty isn't the same thing as total uncertainty.

I think that in the midst of having a million questions, we can forget that the Bible tells us certain things that are

> still to come
> and also
> not uncertain in any way.

> I know the thoughts I think toward you, says the LORD, thoughts of peace and not of evil, to give you a future and a hope. (Jeremiah 29:11)

Life—God's life for us—needs to spring from a vision of future hope. And it may sound like I'm splitting hairs, but we're not hoping in hope; we have a vision of hope. When we hope in hope, we have no assurance of anything, because hope is inanimate. This can lead to more uncertainty and fear and trepidation.

Instead, the Bible gives us a vision of hope—hope that is still to come and is not uncertain in any way. See, hope is not a concept. Hope isn't an idea. Friends, hope has a name because hope is a person.

And His name is Jesus.

We've been seeing this all throughout our journey together. And when we live with a vision of Jesus, we Have Only Positive Expectations. Pay attention to the word *expectations,* because I'm not saying that a vision of Jesus means only positive experiences!

I would never want to give you the wrong impression. I mean, a version of following Jesus that resembles an amusement park—only fun, all the time!—is false hope.

And if you think God is a cosmic vending machine, you will be let down. There's no way around that reality. The Bible teaches us that all sorts of things in life will be hard, challenging, and messy.

But it also teaches that God will work through these things to bring about His will in our lives, which is ultimately beautiful!

I see so many people living right now without a settled confidence in a better future. They are missing the one thing that will give them peace in the storm and bring them out of the tough times with a clear vision for the future God has for them.

I believe that's why the Bible talks about God as the God of all hope.

Look at it this way: We know Jesus.[3] And because we know Him, through His finished work on the cross—His death and resurrection—we should be absolutely overflowing with hope. We should be so drenched with it that others can't help but see it in our lives. And this way of living we

---

[3]   At least I hope you do. If you don't know that you know Jesus, join us on the weekends at https://live.crossroadschurch.net and let's talk more about it!

have been talking about, this positive change, really begins with hope.

HOPE AIN'T EVERYTHING

But I need to remind you that hope is not all we need. By itself, hope isn't enough. We need to marry hope with grit. We need to be willing to go all the way. That idea of grit is a long-term obedience, a perseverance, a stubborn insistence in the direction of our long-term goals.

For those of you who are parents, you know what I'm talking about. Parenting is a gritty reality. It all starts with trying to make it through the pregnancy, and before long you're launching kids out into adulthood! Even then, as they begin to have their own families, parents discover a whole new set of things to deal with along that journey. Parents need to have a stubborn insistence about the direction of their long-term goals for their kids. Parenting without goals and grit is just babysitting.

It's the same with anything that truly matters. Think of your health. Being physically healthy takes hope and grit. From navigating changing metabolism, to unexpected accidents, to the inevitable aging process, it is a journey that must be undertaken with purpose.

This is equally true for fulfilling your God-given purpose. I truly believe that none of us are here by accident and that each of us has our own unique mix of personality, giftings, and passions. But no one ever accomplishes great things without a hope-drenched vision of the future and a ton of grit to see that vision into reality and fulfillment.

The Bible is chock-full of stories of grit, where people

hold on long enough to see the fulfillment of God's promises. I think of the story of Abraham and Sarah and the promised child they waited for . . . until Sarah was ninety years old!

And the story of how it got so real, so quick, when the disciples came to understand that the cross of Jesus had given way to an empty tomb and it was their time to spread the good news.

And in the life of the apostle Paul on his missionary journeys as he endured all sorts of struggles and trials, knowing the gospel would race across the world like wildfire. (Can you even imagine?) Paul was a seriously gritty guy. That's why he can say crazy stuff like how he rejoices in his sufferings (see Colossians 1:24). Hope alone wouldn't have cut it for Paul, and neither would mere human grit. He needed a vision of true, eternal hope, and then he had to have the grit to chase that vision all the way to the end.

I've said that when we are able to marry hope with grit, our lives become unstoppable.

Unstoppable *how*?

I'm talking about the unstoppable future that God has for us as his life is lived through us, where we find ourselves right in the middle of the things that He designed for us—the things only He can reveal and bring to life. And when we're in the middle of all the things God has for us, because His purposes and plans are unstoppable by any human means, His purposes and plans will come to pass in our lives.

The child of God is invincible until God's purposes are complete.

Our lives will be unstoppable once they're no longer our own self-styled lives but rather God's life for us.

In us and through us.

Grace-filled, gritty, and unbelievably good.

WHAT IF?

Close your eyes for a minute and imagine. What if every one of God's kids—me, you, your friends and family, the neighbor or boss you can't stand, the stranger across the world you'll never meet—saw our lives as expressions of the resurrected life of Jesus and we lived our lives that way? What would the world look like?

I have no idea, truly, but I know it would be absolutely mind bending!

The life that God has for us is right there in front of us if we reach out and grab it. Our challenge is to keep our hearts focused on Jesus so we have a hope beyond hope.

And because our eyes are focused on Jesus and we have a clear vision, we live out this internal manifestation of hope at street level, day by day, with a life full of joy-filled grit, perseverance, determination, and steadfastness.

When we put all that together—which is really just the resilient life fueled by hope in Jesus—the inevitable outcome is life. Not because we're unstoppable on our own, but because God's life for us in Christ is unstoppable. Unconquerable.

Incomparable.

So let's get at it!

You can do this!

You're gonna make it!

ACKNOWLEDGMENTS

To Lynn, Obadiah, Maranatha, and Annabelle—I just love and adore you. Thank you for being you and making our family what it is!

To all the Fuscos, Cappadonas, and Dachauers—I love our crazy extended families. I am who I am because of your investment in me.

To the Crossroads family—I am humbled and grateful to walk through life with you all. God is doing so much work in our midst with each passing day. Thank you for simply responding to Jesus together. Pastors Gabriel Moreno and Luke Stillinger deserve a special mention for their efforts in leading Crossroads. Diana Blaser, thank you for all you do! Bob and Heidi Morter for all their faithful work with DFM.

To my writing and publishing team—I love working with you. To D. R. Jacobsen for working so hard on this book. It is such a pleasure to write with you. To Jason Ritchie for all your hard work on the manuscript and for being an exceptional friend. To Alexander Field and the Bindery agency for helping guide me through the publishing process. To everyone at WaterBrook and Multnomah, you have made this such a fun experience. To Paul Pastor, you are not only an amazing editor but also a phenomenal writer and an all-around inspiration to me. To Cara Iverson, thanks for applying your copyediting skills to make this book amazing. To Helen Macdonald for guiding this book through the editing process. To Diane Hobbing for your wonderful design. And to Douglas Mann in Marketing and the amazing people and teams you work with, thank you for helping launch this book.

To Jesus—I just want to tell everyone about You. Thank You for leading me!

Daniel Fusco came to a saving knowledge of Jesus Christ in April 1998 during his last year at Rutgers University, in New Brunswick, New Jersey. After a few years as a professional musician (upright and electric bass), he felt called into pastoral ministry. Soon after, he joined the staff of Calvary Chapel Marin in Novato, California.

After being ordained in 2002, Daniel was sent out to plant Calvary Chapel New Brunswick. In November 2006, he helped raise up another pastor to take his place and moved back to the San Francisco Bay Area to plant more churches. While there, Daniel planted Calvary North Bay in Mill Valley, California. In 2010, while continuing to pastor the church in Mill Valley, he also planted Calvary San Francisco.

In 2012, Daniel turned over both churches to new leadership and moved to Vancouver, Washington, to transition into the lead pastor position at Crossroads Community Church, one of the largest and most well-known churches in the Portland metro area. He has been lead pastor of Crossroads since April 2013.

Daniel's teachings have grown in popularity, which led to the formation of Daniel Fusco Ministries, a nonprofit ministry. His radio program, *Jesus Is Real Radio,* can be heard across the country, and his TV show, *Real with Daniel Fusco,* can be seen weekly on the Hillsong Channel and other networks. Daniel's #2MinuteMessage video series on Facebook has grown his page in amazing ways. You can find his teachings at https://danielfusco.com, YouTube, and wherever you download podcasts.

Daniel has written many books and articles. He self-published his first book, *Ahead of the Curve: Preparing the Church for Post-Postmodernism,* in 2011. In April 2016, he released *Honestly: Getting Real About Jesus and Our Messy Lives* with NavPress. And in October 2017, he published *Upward, Inward, Outward: Love God, Love Yourself, Love Others,* also with NavPress. *Crazy Happy: Nine Surprising Ways to Live the Truly Beautiful Life* was published by Water-Brook in February 2021. Daniel contributes articles to many major outlets, including *USA Today, Preaching Today, Pastors.com, Relevant* magazine, *Leadership Journal, LightWorkers,* and *Faithwire.*

Daniel regularly teaches at churches, conferences, retreats, youth rallies, leadership seminars, seminaries, and college campuses, both in the United States and abroad. His passion for the lost keeps him drinking coffee and playing jazz in and around the great city of Portland, Oregon. He is married to Lynn, and they have three children: Obadiah, Maranatha, and Annabelle.

For more information about Daniel, check out his website at www.danielfusco.com.

God Is Inviting You to Be Crazy Happy

Unlock the happiness you have always longed for in a place that seemed too obvious to look: some of the best-known teachings of Jesus and the apostle Paul. In *Crazy Happy,* you will find God-given beauty that can change your life. You can be crazy happy—even in the midst of our sometimes-crazy world.

DANIEL FUSCO
MINISTRIES

At Daniel Fusco Ministries, we're reaching as many people as possible with the message that life is messy, but Jesus is real. Every week, we hear amazing stories of people who have encountered Jesus for the first time through our ministry. Check out the *Real with Daniel Fusco* TV program on the Hillsong Channel and *Jesus Is Real Radio* over the air or on our daily podcasts. Find out more at **danielfusco.com/stations** and **danielfusco.com/radio**.

Do you want to help us reach more people with the life-changing message of the gospel? We invite you to partner with us and join a special group of people devoted to reaching the world at its places of pain. With the love and life-transforming power of Jesus, we can help them take the next steps in their journey of faith.

Join us at **danielfusco.com/partner**.

More books from Daniel Fusco

| Honestly | Stories Jesus Told | Upward, Inward, Outward |

danielfusco.com

 @danielfusco   @danielfusco   @thefusco

 @thefusco   pastordanielfusco